Illustrated Classics From India

Over 86 million copies of over 400 titles sold worldwide!

Amar Chitra Katha is a collection of illustrated classics that retell stories from Indian mythology, history, folktales and legends through the fascinating medium of comics. Over 430 stories from all over India have been told in this series that has been endorsed by educationists and recommended by teachers the world over.

Through a masterful blend of commentary, dialogue and illustration, Amar Chitra Katha presents complex historical facts and intricate mythology in a format that would appeal to children. They not only entertain, but also provide a fitting introduction to the cultural heritage of India. In a country so vast and varied, the series also serves as a medium for national integration, by introducing young readers to the rich cultural diversity of the country and highlighting the achievements of local heroes.

Amar Chitra Katha comics are like family heirlooms, passed down from generation to generation. These timeless illustrated classics are now also available online on www. amarchitrakatha.com. Start your own collection today!

D1737614

No. 1005 • Rs 195

Amar Chitra Katha Pvt. Ltd.

© Amar Chitra Katha Pvt. Ltd., 1998 , Reprinted January 2008, ISBN 81-89999-50-8
Published & Printed by Amar Chitra Katha Pvt. Ltd., 14, Marthanda, 4th floor,
84, Dr. Annie Besant Road, Mumbai - 400 018. India.

Illustrated Classics From India

Ancestors of Rama

Tradition has it that Rama was the ideal king. Gandhiji was only reinforcing it when he named his ideal state 'Rama-Rajya'. Yet the predecessors of Rama, in his dynasty of the Ikshwakus, were as valiant and as benign as Rama himself. This story tells of their deeds.

The heroes of epics have their tragic flaws because epics always tell the whole truth. Like Rama, his ancestors also had flawed characters despite the glory of their personalities.

Inspired by the epic of Valmiki, Kalidasa wrote his classic poem 'Raghuvamsha'. While chronicling the lives of the ancestors of Rama, it noted the decline of the ruling house also.

It is interesting to note that the puranas trace the geneology of Rama to the Sun. Some of the illustrious ancestors listed in the geneology are Manu, Ikshwaku, Harischandra, Rohita, Sagara, Bhagiratha, Ambarisha and Rituparna, Brihadbala, who fought in the Mahabharata war is said to be a descendant of Rama.

Script : Kamala Chandrakant   Illustrations : Ram Waeerkar   Cover : C.M. Vitankar

AMAR CHITRA KATHA

ANCESTORS OF RAMA

RAMA'S GREAT-GRANDFATHER, THE PIOUS DILIPA OF THE IKSHVAKU RACE, WAS RENOWNED FOR HIS VIRTUE. HIS WIFE SUDAKSHINA WAS DEVOTED TO HIM AND HIS SUBJECTS LOVED HIM. YET HE WAS SAD — HE HAD NO CHILDREN.

ONE DAY, DILIPA HAD AN IDEA.

I SHALL CONSULT SAGE VASISHTHA. HE MAY BE ABLE TO HELP US.

I AM SURE HE WILL.

A FEW DAYS LATER —

I HAVE ENTRUSTED THE KINGDOM TO OUR LOYAL MINISTERS. I AM NOW FREE TO **VISIT** THE SAGE.

AT THE HERMITAGE OF THE SAGE —

I TRUST ALL IS WELL WITH YOU AND YOUR KINGDOM?

BY YOUR GRACE, MY KINGDOM COULD NOT BE MORE PROSPEROUS OR MY SUBJECTS HAPPIER. YET...

...MY QUEEN AND I ARE VERY UNHAPPY. WE YEARN FOR A SON. WHY ARE WE DEPRIVED THUS?

VASISHTHA CLOSED HIS EYES FOR A MOMENT. THEN —

LONG, LONG AGO, WHEN GANGA FLOWED IN HEAVEN, AND YOU WERE A YOUNG PRINCE, YOU HAD GONE TO VISIT INDRA WITH SUDAKSHINA, YOUR CHERISHED BRIDE.

"WHILE RETURNING HOME YOU PASSED BY SURABHI, THE DIVINE COW."

AH! HERE COMES THE CROWN-PRINCE OF AYODHYA WITH HIS BRIDE TO PAY ME HOMAGE. I SHALL BLESS THEM WITH MANY VALIANT SONS.

"YOU WERE SO ENGROSSED IN YOUR YOUNG BRIDE, HOWEVER, THAT YOU HARDLY NOTICED SURABHI. SHE FELT SLIGHTED AND HER INTENDED BLESSING CAME FORTH AS A CURSE."

VAIN PRINCE, MAY YOU AND YOUR BRIDE NEVER HAVE ANY CHILDREN TILL YOU ATONE FOR NEGLEC- TING ME BY SERVING MY OFFSPRING.

"BUT THE DIN OF GANGA WAS SO LOUD THAT YOU DID NOT HEAR THE CURSE, AND DROVE ON."

AS THE WISE WILL TELL YOU, THOSE WHO SLIGHT THE WORTHY, ARE THEMSELVES THE LOSERS.

O VENERABLE ONE, IT WAS AN UNINTENDED SLIGHT. HOW CAN I ATONE FOR IT?

LISTEN. ALONG WITH YOUR WIFE, WAIT ON SURABHI'S DAUGHTER, NANDINI, WITH LOVE AND DEVOTION. PLEASED, NANDINI WILL BESTOW ON YOU THE PRICELESS BOON YOU SEEK.

AT THAT MOMENT, NANDINI CAME BY AND STOOD NEAR THE SAGE.

AT DAWN, SUDAKSHINA MUST ESCORT HER TO THE FOREST AND, IN THE EVENING, WAIT TO WELCOME HER. YOU MUST ATTEND UPON HER DURING THE DAY.

THUS MAY YOU WIN NANDINI'S GRACE AND BECOME THE PROUD FATHER OF MIGHTY SONS.

BEFORE DAWN EACH DAY, SUDAKSHINA WORSHIPPED NANDINI...

...AND LED HER TOWARDS THE EDGE OF THE FOREST.

I SHALL WAIT HERE TO WELCOME HER IN THE EVENING.

FROM DAWN TO DUSK, DILIPA WAITED UPON NANDINI. AS SHE WALKED HE FOLLOWED HER.

WHEN SHE STOPPED, HE STOPPED.

WHILE SHE RESTED, HE TOO RELAXED.

AT DUSK EACH DAY —

AH! MY BELOVED QUEEN! WAITING PATIENTLY, AS USUAL, TO WELCOME NANDINI AND TAKE HER HOME.

AND SO TWENTY-ONE DAYS ROLLED ON.

5

ON THE TWENTY-SECOND DAY, NANDINI WANDERED OUT OF THE FOREST.

THE KING IS PATIENT AND ATTENTIVE. NOW I MUST TEST HIS VALOUR.

UP THE GREEN SLOPES OF THE HIMALAYAS SHE VENTURED...

...INTO SHIVA'S OWN GROVE.

LET HER WANDER. HER INNATE SANCTITY WILL PROTECT HER FROM HARM.

AND DILIPA TURNED TO GAZE AT THE NATURAL SPLENDOUR OF THE SURROUNDINGS. SUDDENLY —

IT'S MY CHARGE! WHO HAS DARED HARM HER!

UM-AW-AW

HE RAN INTO THE GROVE TO FIND NANDINI AT THE MERCY OF A LION.

I'LL SHOOT THE LION AND FREE YOU IN A MOMENT, GENTLE ONE.

BUT TO HIS AMAZEMENT, DILIPA FOUND HIS ARM PARALYZED.

EVEN GREATER WAS HIS AMAZEMENT, WHEN THE LION SPOKE TO HIM.

O KING, I HAVE CAST A SPELL ON YOU. SHIVA HAS POSTED ME HERE TO GUARD THIS TREE, WHICH BOTH PARVATI AND HE LOVE AS A SON. THE COW HAS TRESPASSED. SHE MUST DIE.

NO! I CANNOT LET YOU KILL MY GURU'S COW. KILL ME INSTEAD.

HOW CAN I? IT IS THE COW THAT HAS TRES-PASSED. YOU ONLY FOLLOWED HER LIKE A DEVOTED SON.

AND LIKE A DEVOTED SON I AM WILLING TO GIVE UP MY LIFE FOR HERS.

BY DYING YOU WOULD BE SAVING ONLY ONE LIFE. BUT BY LIVING YOU COULD PROTECT MILLIONS. BESIDES, YOUR DEPENDANTS WOULD BE LOST WITHOUT YOU. SO PRESERVE YOUR VALUABLE LIFE AND RETURN HOME.

WOULD YOU BE ABLE TO FACE SHIVA IF HIS TREE WERE DESTROYED? HOW THEN CAN I BETRAY THE FAITH OF THE VENERABLE SAGE?

DO NOT FEAR THE SAGE. YOU CAN APPEASE HIM WITH GIFTS.

BUT WHAT ABOUT MY HONOUR? I VALUE MY REPUTATION, WHICH WILL LIVE AFTER ME, FAR ABOVE MERE LIFE WHICH IS FLEETING. SO, PLEASE ACCEPT MY OFFER AND LET MY CHARGE GO UNHARMED.

THEN SO BE IT.

AS SOON AS THE LION AGREED, THE SPELL WAS BROKEN AND DILIPA COULD MOVE.

THROWING HIS WEAPONS ASIDE...

...HE FELL BEFORE THE LION EXPECTING DEATH FROM ITS PAWS.

INSTEAD, A SWEET VOICE SOUNDED IN HIS EARS.

RISE, O MY SON!

AS DILIPA SLOWLY ROSE, HE WAS ASTONISHED TO SEE NANDINI WHERE THE LION SHOULD HAVE BEEN.

DO NOT BE AMAZED, O VALIANT KING. I CREATED THIS ILLUSION TO TEST YOU. VASISHTHA'S SPIRITUAL POWER GUARDS ME SO WELL THAT YAMA* HIMSELF CANNOT TOUCH ME.

* THE GOD OF DEATH.

YOUR LOYALTY AND DEVOTION HAVE PLEASED ME. YOU DESERVE A BOON.

THEN, GIVE ME A NOBLE SON, O MOTHER.

SO BE IT!

A FEW DAYS LATER, THE ROYAL COUPLE RETURNED TO THEIR PALACE IN A SWIFT CHARIOT.

THEN, IN DUE TIME, SUDAKSHINA BORE DILIPA A SON.

OUR SON SHALL BE AN INDRA ON EARTH. HIS CHARIOT SHALL RANGE OVER HER REMOTEST BOUNDARIES.

THEN LET US NAME HIM RAGHU, THE SWIFT-MOVING ONE.

SOON, RAGHU WAS OLD ENOUGH TO BEGIN HIS EDUCATION.

TO YOU, THE WISEST IN THE LAND, I ENTRUST THE SPIRITUAL TRAINING OF MY SON.

DILIPA HIMSELF INSTRUCTED RAGHU IN THE ART OF WAR.

RAGHU GREW UP TO BECOME A GENEROUS, NOBLE PRINCE.

AH! MY SON, THE HOPE OF THE KINGDOM! I MUST NOW GET YOU MARRIED AND INSTALL YOU AS THE HEIR-APPARENT.

A FEW YEARS AFTER RAGHU WAS INSTALLED—

MY SON, I PLAN TO PERFORM MY HUNDREDTH SACRIFICE, THE ASHWAMEDHA AND EARN THE TITLE—LORD OF A HUNDRED SACRIFICES WHICH INDRA ALONE NOW ENJOYS. YOU SHALL PROTECT THE SACRIFICIAL HORSE AS IT ROAMS THROUGH THE KINGDOMS OF FRIEND AND FOE.

AS RAGHU AND HIS COMRADES FOLLOWED THE HORSE, THEY DEFEATED AND SUBDUED MANY KINGS.

YOU HAVE DEFEATED ME NOW BUT I SHALL HAVE MY REVENGE.

SOME DAY I SHALL MAKE YOU SUFFER THE SAME HUMILIATION.

MEANWHILE, INDRA, KING OF THE DEVAS, WAS PERTURBED.

IF DILIPA PERFORMS THE ASHWAMEDHA, I WILL NO LONGER HAVE SOLE CLAIM OVER THE TITLE—LORD OF A HUNDRED SACRIFICES.

SO, MAKING HIMSELF INVISIBLE, INDRA DROVE OFF THE HORSE.

THE HORSE! IT'S BEING STOLEN.

BUT I DON'T SEE ANY-BODY!

INDRA, HOWEVER, HAD NOT RECKONED WITH NANDINI'S AFFECTION FOR RAGHU. AS THE PRINCE AND HIS FRIENDS STOOD PERPLEXED, SHE BLESSED HIM WITH SUPERNATURAL VISION.

AH! I HAVE RECEIVED THE GRACE TO SEE THINGS NOT VISIBLE TO THE HUMAN EYE.

AND HE SAW THAT THE THIEF WAS INDRA, KING OF THE DEVAS.

LET THE HORSE GO, O GREAT ONE. YOU SHOULD SMITE OUR FOES - NOT STEAL THE HORSE. YOU KNOW YOU WILL ENJOY A MAJOR SHARE OF THE SACRIFICE. THEN WHY DO YOU HINDER US?

INDRA WAS AMAZED BY RAGHU'S BOLD WORDS. HE STOPPED HIS CHARIOT.

NOBLE PRINCE, YOU SPEAK WELL. BUT BY PERFORMING THE ASHWAMEDHA YOUR FATHER PLANS TO ROB ME OF MY TITLE. I MEAN TO KEEP IT.

IN REPLY RAGHU RAISED HIS BOW AND TOOK AIM.

YOU'LL HAVE TO KILL ME FIRST.

THE ARROW FOUND ITS MARK.

INDRA WAS FURIOUS.

HE PLACED A DEADLY ARROW ON HIS BOW AND TOOK AIM.

BUT RAGHU WAS TOO QUICK FOR HIM.

AND BEFORE INDRA COULD RECOVER FROM THE SHOCK, RAGHU SHOT DOWN HIS FLAG.

HIS THIRD ARROW CUT INDRA'S BOWSTRING IN TWO.

ENRAGED, INDRA FLUNG HIS BOW AWAY AND···

...SEIZING HIS LETHAL WEAPON, VAJRA...

...HURLED IT AT RAGHU.

ALAS! OUR PRINCE HAS FALLEN!

HOW WILL WE FACE THE KING?

BUT LO! THE NEXT MOMENT RAGHU WAS ON HIS FEET AGAIN. INDRA WAS AMAZED.

YOU HAVE WITH-STOOD MY WEAPON, WHICH EVEN MOUN-TAINS CANNOT FACE. I'LL GIVE YOU WHAT-EVER YOU ASK FOR, EXCEPT THE HORSE.

THEN LET MY FATHER BE GIVEN THE FULL MERITS OF ALL HIS SACRIFICES, EVEN THOUGH HE MAY NOT COMPLETE THE HUNDREDTH. AND...LET MY FATHER KNOW THIS BEFORE I REACH AYODHYA.

SO SHALL IT BE.

AND INDRA'S CHARIOT SOARED HEAVENWARDS.

15

INDRA KEPT HIS PROMISE. A PROUD DILIPA STOOD WAITING TO WELCOME THE HERO, AS HE ENTERED AYODHYA IN TRIUMPH.

DEAR SON, INDRA'S MESSENGER SPOKE OF YOUR VALOUR TOO BUT YOUR SCARRED HANDS ARE MORE ELOQUENT.

LATER —

I NOW WISH TO ENTRUST THE KINGDOM TO YOU AND LEAD AN ASCETIC LIFE WITH YOUR MOTHER.

SO RAGHU BECAME KING AND DILIPA, WITH SUDAKSHINA, RETIRED TO THE FORESTS.

MEANWHILE, THE VASSAL KINGS, WHOM RAGHU HAD SUBDUED, NOW ROSE IN REVOLT.

IF YOUR KING WANTS HIS TRIBUTE, LET HIM COME AND GET IT.

. RAGHU MADE A DECISION.

WE SHALL LEAVE ON A CAMPAIGN OF UNIVERSAL CONQUEST. WE WILL NOT RETURN TILL WE HAVE CONQUERED THE EARTH.

HE SET OUT ON THE CAMPAIGN AT THE HEAD OF A HUGE ARMY.

17

A FEW YEARS LATER, HIS MIGHTY MISSION ACCOMPLISHED, A TRIUMPHANT RAGHU MARCHED HOMEWARDS TO AYODHYA.

A HERALD ANNOUNCED HIS ARRIVAL IN THE CITY.

...AND INSTEAD OF THEIR CROWNS THE DUST OF HIS CHARIOT COVERS THEIR HUMBLED HEADS. OUR KING RETURNS WITH UNTOLD WEALTH.

HIS POWER ESTABLISHED, RAGHU NOW DECIDED TO GIVE AWAY ALL HIS WEALTH.

ENOUGH WEALTH SHOULD FIRST BE GIVEN TO ALL THOSE KINGS WHOM I HAVE CONQUERED. THE REST SHOULD BE DISTRIBUTED AMONG MY SUBJECTS.

AS THE LAST LOT OF TREASURES WAS GIVEN AWAY, A YOUNG SAGE STOOD. BEFORE RAGHU.

ALAS! THERE IS NOTHING LEFT.

WELCOME, O SAGE! HOW IS YOUR GURU? WHAT CAN I DO FOR YOU?

ALL IS WELL WITH US, O KING. I HAD COME FOR THE FEE WHICH I HAVE TO PAY TO MY TEACHER. BUT I SEE THAT I HAVE COME TOO LATE. I WILL HAVE TO GO AND TRY ELSEWHERE.

AS THE SAGE TURNED TO GO —

WAIT, O VIRTUOUS ONE. I CANNOT LET YOU DO THAT. WHAT IS YOUR GURU'S DEMAND?

THE SAGE MENTIONED THE AMOUNT.

KUBERA* ALONE NOW POSSESSES SUCH WEALTH. I WILL HAVE TO TAKE IT FROM HIM.

* THE GOD OF WEALTH.

YOU SHALL HAVE THE AMOUNT YOU NEED. BE MY GUEST FOR A FEW DAYS, WHILE I SECURE IT.

THAT NIGHT RAGHU GOT HIS CHARIOT AND WEAPONS READY.

I SHALL INVADE ALAKA-PURI* AT DAWN AND CHALLENGE KUBERA.

WHEN KUBERA DIVINED HIS INTENTIONS, HOWEVER —

I AM NO MATCH FOR RAGHU. I HAD BETTER GIVE HIM THE WEALTH HE NEEDS, BEFORE HE ATTACKS.

AND KUBERA RAINED A SHOWER OF GOLD COINS INTO RAGHU'S COFFERS.

AT DAWN, AS RAGHU WAS ABOUT TO SET OUT —

LORD! WAIT! WHILE YOU SLEPT, THE LORD OF WEALTH HAS FILLED YOUR COFFERS.

* KUBERA'S CAPITAL.

WHEN RAGHU TOLD THE SAGE ABOUT IT, HE WAS AMAZED.

TO ALL GREAT KINGS EARTH GLADLY YIELDS HER WEALTH. HOW GREAT MUST HE BE WHEN HEAVEN ITSELF SHOWERS HIM WITH WEALTH.

O KING, MAY YOU BE BLESSED WITH A SON AS GREAT AS YOU.

AND SO THE PROMISED SON WAS BORN.

HE SHALL BE CALLED AJA, THE UNBORN ONE—ARISEN FROM THE SUPREME SOUL.

AJA GREW UP TO BE AS VIRTUOUS AND VALIANT A SON AS RAGHU WAS TO HIS PARENTS.

MEANWHILE, AT VIDARBHA, INDUMATI, THE SISTER OF KING BHOJA, HAD COME OF AGE.

INDUMATI MUST SOON BE MARRIED. I SHALL HOLD A SWAYAMVARA FOR HER TO WHICH I SHALL INVITE MANY A NOBLE KING AND CHIEF.

THE INVITATION REACHED THE COURT OF RAGHU. HE SENT FOR AJA.

INDUMATI WOULD MAKE A PEERLESS BRIDE. GO TO VIDARBHA AND WIN HER, MY SON.

SO AJA SET OUT WITH A VAST RETINUE.

TOWARDS THE END OF THEIR JOURNEY, AS THEY SET UP CAMP ON THE BANKS OF THE NARMADA...

...AN ANGRY ROGUE ELEPHANT ATTACKED THEM.

AJA RAISED HIS SPEAR...

...AND HURLED IT AT THE ANIMAL.

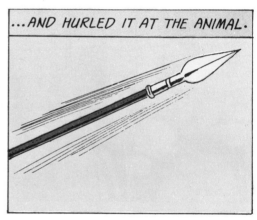

THE MOMENT THE SPEAR PIERCED THE ANIMAL...

...IT TURNED INTO A GANDHARVA.*

YOU HAVE REDEEMED ME FROM A CURSE. AS A REWARD PLEASE ACCEPT THIS MAGIC SPEAR. IT CAN PUT WHOLE ARMIES TO SLEEP.

* A CELESTIAL BEING.

THE NEXT MORNING, AJA AND HIS RETINUE RESUMED THEIR JOURNEY.

THE MEETING WITH THE GANDHARVA TELLS ME THAT I HAVE BEEN FAVOURED. PERHAPS I AM FATED TO WIN THE FAIR BRIDE.

AT VIDARBHA, BHOJA HIMSELF CAME OUT TO RECEIVE AJA.

WELCOME, O SON OF RAGHU. YOU MAY REST TONIGHT AT THE SPECIAL PALACE I HAVE BUILT FOR YOU. MY MEN WILL GUIDE YOU TO YOUR THRONE AT THE SWAYAM-VARA HALL TOMORROW.

THE NEXT MORNING, AS AJA ENTERED THE HALL —

THE SON OF RAGHU!

OH, THAT HE WERE NOT HERE!

WHAT HOPE DO WE HAVE NOW OF WIN-NING THE FAIR BRIDE?

THE AIR WAS TENSE AS THE MIGHTY KINGS AWAITED HER ENTRY—EACH WITH THE HOPE THAT HE WOULD BE THE CHOSEN LORD.

SOON, THE PALANQUIN BEARING INDUMATI WAS BROUGHT IN.

ALL EYES TURNED TO GAZE AT HER. SUNANDA, A ROYAL MATRON, LED HER TO THE KINGS.

THE VALIANT AND PIOUS LORD OF MAGADHA.

NOT THIS ONE.

THUS INDUMATI PASSED EACH HOPEFUL KING BY.

THE HANDSOME KING OF ANGA, WORTHY OF ALL LOVE.

NOT MINE.

THE DEVOUT KING OF AVANTI, WHO IN LOOKS AND VALOUR RIVALS THE VERY DEVAS.

NOT IN MY EYES. LET US MOVE ON.

AT LAST, SHE STOOD BEFORE AJA.

AJA, THE CROWN PRINCE OF AYODHYA, MIGHTY RAGHU'S SON.

INDUMATI MADE NO COMMENT BUT ONLY BLUSHED IN CONFUSION.

HE IS THE CHOSEN ONE. I SHALL TEASE HER.

SHALL WE PASS ON, MY PRINCESS?

INDUMATI HARDLY HEARD HER. WITH HER GAZE STILL LOCKED IN HIS, SHE PLACED THE GARLAND AROUND AJA'S NECK. THERE WAS A ROAR OF APPROVAL FROM THE ASSEMBLY.

GANGA HAS BECOME ONE WITH HER FIT MATE, THE OCEAN.

WHILE THE RIVAL SUITORS LOOKED WITH HOSTILITY AT THE PAIR, KING BHOJA LED INDUMATI AND AJA THROUGH THE FESTIVE CITY.

RAGHU ONCE MERCI- LESSLY HUMBLED US AND NOW HIS SON WALKS OFF WITH OUR PRIZE.

WE MUST AVENGE THE INSULT.

LET US WAYLAY THEM AS THEY RETURN TO AYODHYA.

THREE DAYS LATER, AJA AND HIS BRIDE SET OUT FOR AYODHYA.

SUDDENLY —

AN ARROW! IT'S AN AMBUSH! THE DISAPPOINTED SUITORS!

LORD!

TAKE COURAGE, TIMID ONE. AJA SHALL NOT LOSE YOU, HIS VERY LIFE.

HE TURNED TO AN OLD AND EXPERIENCED COURTIER.

I ENTRUST MY BRIDE TO YOU. GUARD HER WHILE WE MOUNT THE COUNTER-ATTACK.

HIS BRIDE IN SAFE HANDS, AJA TURNED ON HIS FOES.

CHARGE!

FOR A WHILE HE LET THE BATTLE RAGE ON.

THEN, WEARY OF BLOODSHED AND SLAUGHTER, AJA MADE A DECISION.

I SHALL NOW USE MY MAGIC SPEAR.

AT ONCE, THE BEWILDERED KINGS AND THEIR ARMIES WERE CHARMED INTO SLEEP. THE NOISE AND CONFUSION OF BATTLE WAS STILLED.

AJA BLEW HIS CONCH TO ANNOUNCE HIS VICTORY.

THEN HE WENT TO INDUMATI.

COME. BEHOLD OUR FOES. COULD SUCH AS THEY EVER HOPE TO ROB ME OF YOU?

AND THEY RESUMED THEIR JOURNEY TO AYODHYA.

THE MIGHTY KING, MY FATHER WILL REJOICE WHEN HE HEARS OF OUR VICTORY OVER HIS MOST POWERFUL VASSALS.

WHEN THEY REACHED AYODHYA—

NEWS OF YOUR VALOUR HAS TRAVELLED HOME BEFORE YOU. COME, MY CHILDREN, THE ROYAL HOUSEHOLD WAITS TO HONOUR YOU.

LATER—

MY SON, I AM OLD NOW AND WOULD LIKE TO RENOUNCE THE WORLD. BECOME THE SOVEREIGN AND RULE THE COUNTRY IN THE TRADITION OF YOUR ANCESTORS.

AND RAGHU TOOK TO A LIFE OF AUSTERITY AND MEDITATION.

AJA WAS A JUST, WISE AND STRONG KING AND EARNED THE SAME LOVE AND RESPECT FROM HIS SUBJECTS THAT HIS FATHER HAD ENJOYED.

ALL THAT AYODHYA NOW NEEDS IS AN HEIR AS PIOUS AND VALIANT AS OUR KING.

AND THAT HOPE TOO WAS SOON FULFILLED WHEN A SON WAS BORN TO INDUMATI— THE SON WHO BECAME KNOWN AS DASHARATHA, THE FATHER OF RAMA.

Dasharatha

The Story of Rama's Father

AMAR
CHITRA
KATHA

Illustrated Classics From India

Dasharatha

This Amar Chitra Katha has been drawn mainly from Valmiki's famous epic poem – Ramayana.

Ravana, an evil Rakshasa had performed severe penances and obtained a boon from Brahma. No celestial being, be it a yaksha, a gandharva or deva, could kill him. Armed with this boon, he invaded Amaravati, the city of the devas and played haveoc among its inhabitants. Distressed, they appealed to Vishnu. On earth at that time, Dasharatha, the prosperous, wise and just king of Ayodhya bent on obtaining a son, was engaged in performing a series of sacrifices. To help the devas, Vishnu decided to manifest himself on earth and destroy Ravana, since Brahma's boon did not protect Ravana from men. He chose to be born as four sons to three queens of Dasharatha. As Dasharatha delighted in his growing sons, particularly in Rama, the eldest, little did he dream that a curse, hurled at him when he was a mere lad would result in his death.

Script : Kamala Chandrakant   Illustrations : M.N. Nangare   Cover : Pratap Mulick

DASHARATHA

DASHARATHA, THE SON OF AJA AND INDUMATI, WAS THE BELOVED CROWN PRINCE OF AYODHYA, THE CAPITAL OF THE FLOURISHING KINGDOM OF KOSALA ON THE BANKS OF THE RIVER SARAYU. LIKE HIS FATHER, YOUNG DASHARATHA WAS A SKILFUL ARCHER. HE COULD HIT HIS TARGET GUIDED ONLY BY SOUND. AND HE LOVED TO EXERCISE THIS SKILL.

ONE DARK, RAINY NIGHT AS DASHARATHA WAS LOOKING OUT FOR GAME—

GLUG GLUG GLUG GLUG GLUG GLUG

WHAT'S THAT? A THIRSTY ELEPHANT'S TRUNK, OUT FOR ITS FILL!

1

HE AIMED AT THE SOUND AND LET HIS DEADLY ARROW FLY. WHEN THE ARROW FOUND ITS MARK—

AH! MURDER. BUT I HAVE HARMED NONE. AH! MY POOR, OLD, BLIND PARENTS! I LEAVE YOU, HELPLESS.

DASHARATHA HAD MISTAKEN THE GURGLE OF THE HERMIT'S FILLING PITCHER FOR THE SOUND OF AN ELEPHANT DRINKING WATER.

FOR A MOMENT HE STOOD PETRIFIED.

WHAT HAVE I DONE! I WHO AM A VIRTUOUS KOSALA PRINCE, THE PROTECTOR OF THE WEAK!

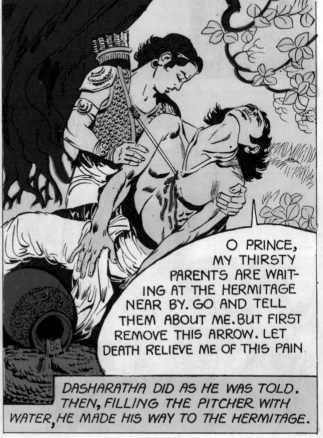

THEN, HE RAN TO THE SPOT FROM WHERE THE HUMAN CRY HAD COME. AS SOON AS THE DYING YOUTH SAW HIM —

O PRINCE, MY THIRSTY PARENTS ARE WAITING AT THE HERMITAGE NEAR BY. GO AND TELL THEM ABOUT ME. BUT FIRST REMOVE THIS ARROW. LET DEATH RELIEVE ME OF THIS PAIN.

DASHARATHA DID AS HE WAS TOLD. THEN, FILLING THE PITCHER WITH WATER, HE MADE HIS WAY TO THE HERMITAGE.

MEANWHILE, AT THE HERMITAGE —

OUR SON HAS BEEN AWAY A LONG WHILE. COULD SOMETHING HAVE HAPPENED TO HIM?

JUST THEN THEY HEARD FOOTSTEPS APPROACHING.

AH! THERE YOU ARE AT LAST. QUICK, GIVE ME THE WATER. I CANNOT BEAR THE THIRST ANY LONGER.

TEARS FLOWED DOWN DASHARATHA'S FACE AS HE STOOD THERE, SPEECHLESS WITH GUILT.

WHY ARE YOU SILENT, MY SON? YOU KNOW THAT YOU ARE OUR VERY LIFE. SPEAK TO US, DEAR SON.

O VENERABLE ONE, I AM NOT YOUR SON. MY NAME IS DASHARATHA. I HAVE COMMITTED A HEINOUS SIN AND STAND BEFORE YOU, SAD AND REPENTANT.

AND DASHARATHA TOLD THEM WHAT HE HAD UNKNOWINGLY DONE.

THE OLD COUPLE SAT STUNNED FOR A FEW SECONDS. THEN PAST THE CHOKING GRIEF CAME THE WORDS.

IT WAS MY SON. OUR ONLY SON. YOU KILLED HIM.

THE BEREFT FATHER CURSED DASHARATHA.

YOUR SON TOO SHALL BE PARTED FROM YOU. AND YOU SHALL DIE GRIEVING FOR HIM.

A THOROUGHLY SHAKEN DASHARATHA RETURNED TO HIS PALACE.

BUT THE INCIDENT GRADUALLY FADED FROM HIS MEMORY. ONE DAY AJA SENT FOR HIM.

DASHARATHA, EVER SINCE YOUR MOTHER DIED THE KINGDOM HAS BECOME A BURDEN TO ME. YOU HAVE COME OF AGE. NOW YOU RULE THE LAND AND LET ME RETIRE TO THE FOREST.

SOON AFTER, ON THE ADVICE OF HIS MINISTERS AND SPIRITUAL GUIDES, DASHARATHA MARRIED KAUSALYA, A PRINCESS OF KOSALA.

DASHARATHA WAS A NOBLE, VIRTUOUS KING AND WAS LOVED BY ALL. SO RENOWNED FOR VALOUR WAS HE THAT EVEN INDRA, KING OF THE DEVAS, SOUGHT HIS HELP IN HIS WARS WITH THE ASURAS.

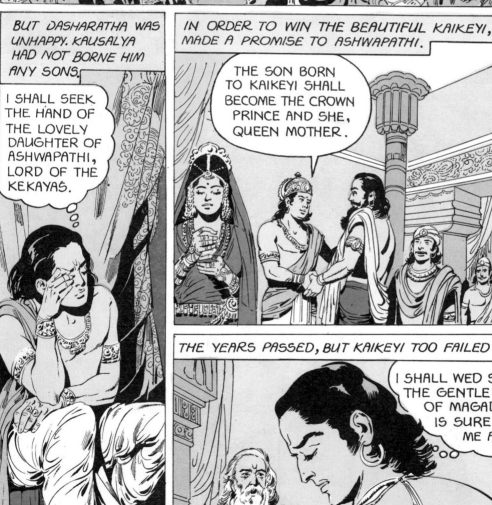

BUT DASHARATHA WAS UNHAPPY. KAUSALYA HAD NOT BORNE HIM ANY SONS.

I SHALL SEEK THE HAND OF THE LOVELY DAUGHTER OF ASHWAPATHI, LORD OF THE KEKAYAS.

IN ORDER TO WIN THE BEAUTIFUL KAIKEYI, DASHARATHA MADE A PROMISE TO ASHWAPATHI.

THE SON BORN TO KAIKEYI SHALL BECOME THE CROWN PRINCE AND SHE, QUEEN MOTHER.

THE YEARS PASSED, BUT KAIKEYI TOO FAILED HIM.

I SHALL WED SUMITRA, THE GENTLE PRINCESS OF MAGADHA. SHE IS SURE TO BEAR ME A SON.

BUT SUMITRA TOO REMAINED A BARREN WIFE.

MEANWHILE INDRA, KING OF THE DEVAS, WAS IN TROUBLE ONCE AGAIN. ONE DAY—

O KING, LORD INDRA SEEKS YOUR HELP AGAINST THE ASURA SHAMBARA.

DASHARATHA TURNED TO KAIKEYI.

I SHALL LEAVE IMMEDIATELY.

LORD, LET ME COME WITH YOU.

HA, HA, MY DEAR ONE, A BATTLEFIELD IS NO PLACE FOR YOU.

BUT I AM NO ORDINARY WOMAN. I AM THE DAUGHTER OF THE INVINCIBLE ASHWA-PATHI.

BESIDES, MY LORD, I DO NOT WISH TO BE HERE ALONE WITHOUT YOU.

THEN COME, LOVABLE ONE. COME WITH ME TO THE BATTLE-FIELD.

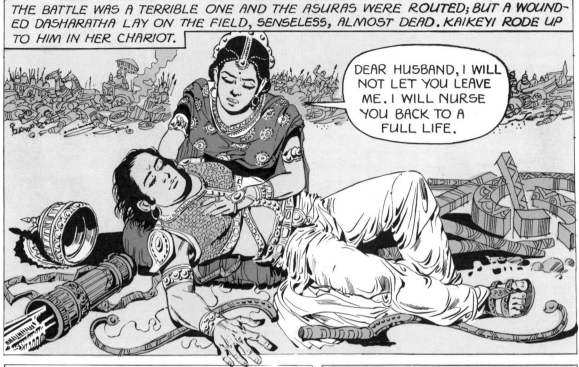

THE BATTLE WAS A TERRIBLE ONE AND THE ASURAS WERE *ROUTED*; BUT A WOUND-ED DASHARATHA LAY ON THE FIELD, SENSELESS, ALMOST DEAD. KAIKEYI RODE UP TO HIM IN HER CHARIOT.

DEAR HUSBAND, I WILL NOT LET YOU LEAVE ME. I WILL NURSE YOU BACK TO A FULL LIFE.

SHE HAD HIM REMOVED TO HER TENT AND TENDED HIM DAY AND NIGHT TILL HE REGAINED CONSCIOUSNESS. AS SOON AS HE OPENED HIS EYES—

KAIKEYI, MY DEAREST QUEEN, YOU HAVE BROUGHT ME BACK TO LIFE. ASK ANY TWO BOONS OF ME.

AT THIS MOMENT, WITH YOU ALIVE, I HAVE ALL I NEED, MY LORD. I'LL ASK FOR THE BOONS WHEN I NEED THEM.

FROM THEN ON KAIKEYI BECAME DASHARATHA'S FAVOURITE QUEEN. THE GENTLE YOUNG SUMITRA, UNABLE TO BEAR HIS NEGLECT, SPOKE HER HEART OUT TO KAUSALYA WHOSE SPE-CIAL PROTECTION SHE ENJOYED.

EVER SINCE THE BOLD KAIKEYI ACCOMPANIED OUR LORD TO THE BATTLE-FIELD, HE HAS NO EYES FOR US. IT HURTS ME.

NEVER MIND, SUMITRA. LET US CONTINUE TO SERVE HIM WITH LOVE AND DEVOTION.

SUCH INFATUATIONS DO NOT LAST LONG. PERHAPS ONLY TILL ONE OF US BEARS HIM A SON.

BUT NONE OF THE THREE QUEENS BORE DASHARATHA A SON. AS THE YEARS PASSED, DASHARATHA'S YEARNING FOR A SON GREW. AT LAST—

I SHALL PERFORM A SACRIFICE AND OBTAIN A SON TO RULE THE KINGDOM.

ORDERS WERE GIVEN AND ALL WERE READY FOR THE GRAND SACRIFICE. AS THE SACRIFICIAL FIRE BLAZED, A BEING HOLDING A BOWL OF 'PAYASA'*, SUDDENLY EMERGED FROM IT.

O KING, GIVE THIS TO YOUR WORTHY QUEENS AND THEY SHALL BEAR YOU SONS.

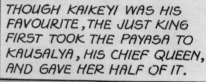

THOUGH KAIKEYI WAS HIS FAVOURITE, THE JUST KING FIRST TOOK THE PAYASA TO KAUSALYA, HIS CHIEF QUEEN, AND GAVE HER HALF OF IT.

PARTAKE OF THIS DEAR WIFE, AND BEAR ME A SON.

* A GRUEL MADE OUT OF MILK, SUGAR AND RICE.

THEN HE WENT TO SUMITRA AND GAVE HER A FOURTH OF WHAT WAS LEFT.

I SHALL GIVE THE REST TO KAIKEYI.

AS HE WAS ABOUT TO DO SO, A THOUGHT SUDDENLY STRUCK HIM AND HE CHANGED HIS MIND.

I SHALL GIVE HER ONLY HALF OF IT AND GIVE THE REST TO GENTLE SUMITRA.

WITHIN A YEAR, KAUSALYA GAVE BIRTH TO RAMA; KAIKEYI TO BHARATA, AND SUMITRA, WHO HAD THE 'PAYASA' TWICE, TO LAKSHMANA AND SHATRUGHNA. THOUGH THE PRINCES LOVED EACH OTHER—

RAMA IS DEARER TO LAKSHMANA THAN LIFE ITSELF. AND SHATRUGHNA IS PARTIAL TO BHARATA. I WAS WISE TO GIVE THE DOCILE SUMITRA THE SECOND PORTION.

AND THOUGH ALL FOUR PRINCES DELIGHTED THE HEART OF DASHARATHA, RAMA, THE ELDEST, WAS HIS FAVOURITE. INDEED, HE WAS THE FAVOURITE OF ALL AYODHYA.

HE HAS EVEN BECOME THE FAVOURITE OF KAIKEYI AND SUMITRA FOR HE LOVES AND HONOURS THEM AS HE DOES HIS OWN MOTHER. HE WOULD MAKE AN IDEAL KING FOR AYODHYA.

BUT I AM BOUND BY MY PROMISE TO KAIKEYI'S FATHER WHEN I MARRIED HER.

A FEW DAYS LATER—

HOW WELL BHARATA SHOOTS! KAIKEYI, MY BELOVED, HE WILL MAKE AN EXCELLENT KING.

YES, MY LORD. BUT RAMA IS OUR ELDEST SON AND IS AN IDEAL PRINCE. BESIDES HE LOVES ME EVEN MORE THAN HIS OWN MOTHER.

DASHARATHA WAS HAPPY TO HEAR THIS.

HER WORDS REASSURE ME AS I WOULD HAVE RAMA RULE AFTER ME. YET, I MUST TAKE CARE TO KEEP KAIKEYI IN THIS FRAME OF MIND.

STRIVING TO KEEP KAIKEYI HAPPY ALWAYS, DASHARATHA NEGLECTED KAUSALYA AND SUMITRA.

SENSING REJECTION AS WIFE, KAUSALYA MAGNIFIED HER ROLE AS HOUSEWIFE. ONE DAY AS SHE EXAMINED THE EXPENSES OF THE QUEENS' APARTMENTS—

KAIKEYI SPENDS MORE THAN WE DO. IF ONLY THE KING WOULDN'T INDULGE HER SO.

10

SHE SENT FOR THE YOUNGER QUEEN.

KAIKEYI, EXTRAVAGANCE IS BAD; EVEN IN REGAL QUARTERS.

MY APARTMENTS AND MY PERSON MUST BE WORTHY OF MY LORD, THE KING. MORE SO AS HE SPENDS MOST OF HIS LEISURE HOURS WITH ME.

THE TAUNT HURT KAUSALYA BUT SHE WISELY MAINTAINED HER SILENCE.

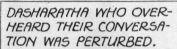

DASHARATHA WHO OVER-HEARD THEIR CONVERSA-TION WAS PERTURBED.

THEIR QUARRELS SHOULD NOT SPOIL RAMA'S CHANCES. I MUST ENSURE THAT SUCH SITUATIONS DO NOT COME UP AGAIN.

MEANWHILE THE CHILDREN HAD GROWN INTO HANDSOME YOUTHS.

IT IS TIME THE PRINCES WERE MARRIED.

JUST THEN—

LORD, THE RENOWNED SAGE, VISHWA-MITRA, IS HERE.

DASHARATHA AND THE OTHERS RUSHED OUT TO WELCOME THE SAGE.

LATER—

O VENERABLE ONE, CAN I BE OF ANY SERVICE TO YOU? I PROMISE TO GRANT ANY WISH OF YOURS.

O KING, CERTAIN RAK-SHASAS* FREQUENT-LY SPOIL MY SACRED RITUALS.

SEND YOUR ELDEST SON, THE VALIANT RAMA, WITH ME. ONLY HE CAN DESTROY THEM.

DASHARATHA WAS STUNNED. HE COULD HARDLY SPEAK.

RAMA IS BARELY SIXTEEN, A MERE BOY. NO! I CANNOT PART WITH MY FIRST-BORN. IF YOU LIKE, MY FRIENDS AND I WILL HELP YOU.

VISHWAMITRA WAS ENRAGED.

O KING, YOUR WORDS ARE UNWORTHY OF YOUR LINEAGE. YOU GAVE ME A PROMISE AND NOW SAY YOU CANNOT KEEP IT.

* DEMONS

AS THE ANGRY SAGE WAS ABOUT TO STOMP OUT, VASISHTA, DASHARATHA'S SPIRITUAL GUIDE, TURNED TO THE KING.

THEN LET LAKSHMANA GO WITH RAMA.

KEEP YOUR WORD. SEND RAMA. THIS MIGHTY SAGE CAN BRING NOTHING BUT GOOD FOR YOUR SON.

SO RAMA AND LAKSHMANA WENT WITH VISHWAMITRA.

A FEW DAYS LATER, ENVOYS FROM THE COURT OF JANAKA, THE KING OF MITHILA, CAME TO THE COURT OF DASHARATHA.

WE BRING GLAD TIDINGS. SITA, THE DAUGHTER OF OUR VALIANT KING, HAS BEEN WON BY RAMA. OUR KING AWAITS YOUR PLEASURE AND INVITES YOU THERE.

WE COULD NOT HAVE HOPED FOR A BETTER ALLIANCE.

AN EXCELLENT PROPOSAL!

THEN LET US PROCEED EARLY TOMORROW. WE'LL TAKE BHARATA AND SHATRUGHNA WITH US.

AT MITHILA, JANAKA AND HIS YOUNGER BROTHER GAVE THEM A ROYAL WELCOME. LATER —

IF YOU ARE AGREEABLE I WOULD GLADLY HAVE MY SECOND DAUGHTER, URMILA, WED LAKSHMANA.

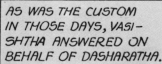

AS WAS THE CUSTOM IN THOSE DAYS, VASI-SHTHA ANSWERED ON BEHALF OF DASHARATHA.

JANAKA WAS OVERJOYED.

THEN LET THE FOUR PRINCES BE MARRIED ON THE SAME DAY. THE ROYAL FAMILIES OF KOSALA AND MITHILA SHALL PROSPER IN THE UNION.

THE PROPOSAL IS ACCEPTED. IF YOU ARE WILLING WE WOULD ALSO ACCEPT YOUR YOUNGER BROTHER'S DAUGHTERS FOR BHARATA AND SHATRUGHNA.

WHILE THE PREPARATIONS FOR THE WEDDINGS WERE GOING ON, KAIKEYI'S BROTHER, YUDDHAJIT, CAME TO MITHILA AND PRESENTED HIMSELF BEFORE DASHARATHA.

MY FATHER SENT ME TO AYODHYA TO TAKE BHARATA TO OUR KINGDOM FOR A FEW YEARS. I HEARD THE NEWS THERE AND FOLLOW-ED YOU TO MITHILA.

WELCOME, YUDDHA-JIT. IT IS FORTU-NATE THAT YOU ARE HERE NOW.

AS SOON AS THE ARRANGEMENTS WERE OVER, AN AUSPICIOUS DAY WAS FIXED AND THE NUPTIALS PERFORMED.

DASHARATHA AND THE YOUNG COUPLES RETURNED TO A JUBILANT AYODHYA. AT THE PALACE, DASHARATHA'S WIVES STOOD JOYOUS AND EXPECTANT.

WELCOME, DEAR DAUGHTERS. MAY YOU KNOW ONLY HAPPINESS IN YOUR NEW HOME.

A FEW MONTHS LATER, DASHARATHA SENT FOR BHARATA.

YOU MAY NOW GO WITH YOUR UNCLE TO YOUR GRAND-FATHER.

AS THE YEARS WENT BY, RAMA'S EXCELLENCE, NOW AS A HOUSEHOLDER, ENDEARED HIM EVEN MORE TO THE AGE-ING KING. ONE DAY—

I SHALL SEE RAMA CROWNED YUVRAJA, WITHOUT ANY DELAY. I SHALL ANNOUNCE MY DECISION AT AN ASSEMBLY OF ELDERS, KINGS AND WISE MEN.

DASHARATHA SOON MADE HIS WISH KNOWN TO HIS COUNSELLORS. THEN—

...AND AS TIME IS RUNNING OUT THERE IS LITTLE NEED TO INVITE ASHWAPATHI AND JANAKA TO THE CORONATION.

15

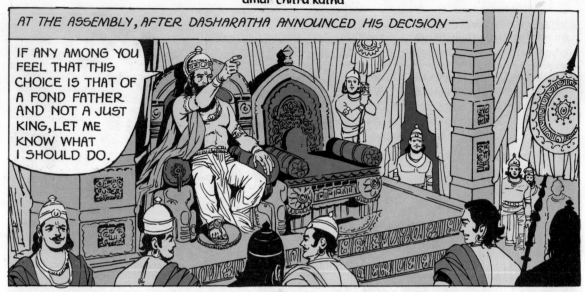

AT THE ASSEMBLY, AFTER DASHARATHA ANNOUNCED HIS DECISION—

IF ANY AMONG YOU FEEL THAT THIS CHOICE IS THAT OF A FOND FATHER AND NOT A JUST KING, LET ME KNOW WHAT I SHOULD DO.

THE KINGS AND SAGES AT THE SABHA WEIGHED THE MATTER CAREFULLY. THEN—

O JUST KING, INSTALL RAMA AS THE HEIR-APPARENT. WE, THE PEOPLE, LOOK FORWARD TO IT.

DASHARATHA WAS PLEASED. HE TURNED TO SUMANTRA, HIS FAVOURITE COUNSELLOR.

BRING RAMA HITHER.

A LITTLE LATER RAMA ENTERED THE ASSEMBLY.

THE KING EMBRACED HIM AND MADE HIM SIT ON A THRONE, SPECIALLY MADE FOR HIM, NEXT TO HIS OWN.

WE, THE KING AND THE PEOPLE, PROPOSE TO INSTALL YOU AS THE HEIR-APPARENT.

THE ANNOUNCEMENT OVER, RAMA RETURNED TO HIS OWN CHAMBER. LATER—

THE KING WOULD LIKE TO SEE YOU ALONE.

HAVE THE PEOPLE PROMPTED THE KING TO REVERSE A HASTY DECISION? WELL, WHATEVER HAPPENS IS FOR THE BEST.

PREPARED FOR THE WORST, RAMA STOOD BEFORE DASHARATHA. BUT—

MY SON, I HAVE DECIDED TO HAVE YOU INSTALLED TOMORROW ITSELF. LET YOUR FRIENDS PROTECT YOU WELL TONIGHT. FOR, MANY ARE THE HAZARDS THAT THREATEN AFFAIRS LIKE THIS.

RAMA LOOKED UP, AMAZED.

BUT BHARATA IS AWAY FROM THE CAPITAL...

WHICH IN MY OPINION MAKES THE TIME MOST OPPORTUNE FOR YOUR INSTALLATION.

BUT FATHER, BHARATA IS VIRTUOUS AND...

THE MINDS OF EVEN RIGHTEOUS AND DEVOUT MEN ARE INCONSTANT. SO YOUR CORONATION MUST BE HELD TOMORROW. YOU MAY GO NOW.

WHEN THE NEWS REACHED KAUSALYA—

MAY MY GLORIOUS SON LIVE LONG. HERE, ACCEPT THESE FOR BRINGING SUCH AUSPICIOUS TIDINGS.

MANTHARA, KAIKEYI'S HUNCH-BACKED CHILDHOOD NURSE AND CONFIDANTE, HAPPENED TO SEE THIS.

WHAT! THE THRIFTY KAUSALYA GIVING AWAY GEMS AND GOLD!

SHE TURNED TO A MAID NEAR BY.

WHY IS THE CHIEF QUEEN SO HAPPY?

RAMA HAS BEEN ELECTED HEIR-APPARENT.

MANTHARA WAS SHOCKED.

BUT HADN'T DASHARATHA PROMISED THE KINGDOM TO MY KAIKEYI'S SON? I MUST INFORM HER OF THE TREACHERY AFOOT.

18

A LITTLE LATER, RAMA CAME TO HIS MOTHER'S APARTMENTS. SUMITRA, LAKSHMANA AND SITA WERE ALREADY THERE.

MOTHER, THE PRIESTS SAY THAT SITA MUST FAST WITH ME TONIGHT. PLEASE ARRANGE ALL THAT WE WILL NEED FOR IT.

KAUSALYA TREMBLED WITH DELIGHT TO HEAR THE WORDS SHE HAD EVER HOPED TO HEAR.

O RAMA, YOU MUST PLEASE THE HEARTS OF SUMITRA'S SONS TOO.

LAKSHMANA, MY LIFE AND THIS KINGDOM, TOO, ARE YOURS. RULE WITH ME.

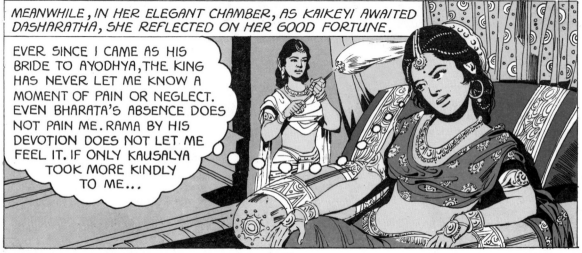

MEANWHILE, IN HER ELEGANT CHAMBER, AS KAIKEYI AWAITED DASHARATHA, SHE REFLECTED ON HER GOOD FORTUNE.

EVER SINCE I CAME AS HIS BRIDE TO AYODHYA, THE KING HAS NEVER LET ME KNOW A MOMENT OF PAIN OR NEGLECT. EVEN BHARATA'S ABSENCE DOES NOT PAIN ME. RAMA BY HIS DEVOTION DOES NOT LET ME FEEL IT. IF ONLY KAUSALYA TOOK MORE KINDLY TO ME...

19

HER PLEASANT MUSINGS WERE RUDELY INTERRUPTED BY MANTHARA'S RAUCOUS VOICE.

WAKE UP, KAIKEYI! YOUR GOOD DAYS ARE ABOUT TO COME TO A RUDE END.

WHY, MANTHARA! YOU ARE PALE. WHAT'S THE MATTER? IS ALL WELL WITH MY LORD?

THE LORD IS IN HIS HEAVEN BUT ALL IS ILL WITH YOU. O MY INNOCENT ONE, THE CRAFTY KING HAS SENT YOUR SON AWAY, ONLY TO INSTALL HIS RAMA AS THE HEIR-APPARENT.

KAIKEYI'S FACE LIT UP.

MY VIRTUOUS RAMA? HEIR-APPARENT? YOU HAVE BROUGHT ME HAPPY NEWS.

SHE TOOK OFF HER NECKLACE AND—

HERE, TAKE THIS. ASK FOR ANY OTHER REWARD AND IT SHALL BE YOURS.

A DISGUSTED MANTHARA FLUNG THE ORNAMENT ASIDE.

DON'T YOU UNDERSTAND? WITH HER SON AS THE HEIR-APPARENT, KAUSALYA WILL HUMILIATE YOU. SHE HAS A LONG MEMORY.

RAMA WILL NOT LET HER. BESIDES, IF THE KINGDOM BE RAMA'S IT WILL BE BHARATA'S TOO. RAMA IS ABOVE PETTY DISTINCTIONS.

MANTHARA BREATHED HARD WITH EXASPERATION.

IMPOSSIBLE! THE CORONATION OF RAMA WILL CUT BHARATA OFF THE ROYAL LINE FOR EVER. IT IS YOUR DUTY AS A KSHATRIYA MOTHER TO PROTECT THE ROYAL RIGHTS OF YOUR SON AND HIS DEPENDANTS.

I HAD NOT THOUGHT OF THAT!

YES, WHEN RAMA BECOMES KING, HE WILL BANISH BHARATA OR KILL HIM. THEN, MY HAUGHTY ONE, YOU WILL BE A SLAVE IN THE ROYAL HOUSEHOLD. HAVE NO DOUBTS ABOUT IT.

NO! NEVER!

MY SON MUST BECOME THE KING. THIS VERY DAY I WILL SEND RAMA TO THE FOREST AND INSTALL BHARATA ON THE THRONE.

AH, KAIKEYI! LISTEN TO ME THEN.

REMEMBER THE TWO BOONS DASHARATHA HAD OFFERED YOU MANY YEARS AGO.

ASK FOR THEM NOW. ASK FOR THE INSTALLATION OF BHARATA AND THE EXILE OF RAMA FOR FOURTEEN YEARS. BY THAT TIME BHARATA CAN BE A POPULAR KING AND AN INVINCIBLE MONARCH.

WHEN SHALL I DEMAND THE BOONS?

NOW! CAST OFF YOUR FINERY AND ENTER THE CHAMBER OF PROTEST. DO NOT SPEAK TO THE KING WHEN YOU SEE HIM. LET ONLY YOUR TEARS FLOW, UNCONTROLLED, LET YOUR SOBS WRENCH HIS HEART.

A FEW MINUTES LATER—

YOU HAVE ALWAYS BEEN HIS FAVOURITE. SO BE BOLD AND ACHIEVE YOUR ENDS.

HOW WISE YOU ARE, MANTHARA! I WOULD NEVER HAVE SUSPECTED THE KING'S MOTIVES. YOU SHALL HAVE ALL THE POWER AND MONEY YOU WANT WHEN BHARATA IS INSTALLED.

AT THAT MOMENT, DASHARATHA WAS ON HIS WAY TO THE QUEEN'S APARTMENTS.

I WILL GO TO KAIKEYI FIRST. SHE HAD ALWAYS SEEN THE HEIR-APPARENT IN RAMA.

BUT—

THIS IS UNUSUAL. KAIKEYI AWAY FROM HER CHAMBER? AT THIS HOUR?

WHERE IS QUEEN KAIKEYI?

IN THE CHAMBER OF PROTEST, YOUR MAJESTY.

IN THE CHAMBER OF PROTEST? TILL TODAY NOT ONE OF MY QUEENS HAS FOUND THE NEED TO USE IT.

DASHARATHA HURRIED THERE. HE WAS AMAZED AND DISTRESSED BY WHAT HE SAW.

O KAIKEYI, WHY ARE YOU IN TEARS? TELL ME WHY YOU ARE SAD. I'LL IMME-DIATELY SET MATTERS RIGHT.

HAS ANYONE OFFENDED YOU? HAS ANYONE REPRI-MANDED YOU?

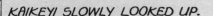

KAIKEYI SLOWLY LOOKED UP.

NO, MY LORD. I WANT SOMETHING DONE. IF YOU PROMISE TO DO IT, I WILL SPEAK.

YOU KNOW THAT EXCEPT RAMA WHO IS MY VERY LIFE, THERE IS NO ONE DEARER TO ME THAN YOU. I SWEAR BY RAMA THAT I WILL DO WHATEVER YOU WANT.

REMEMBER THE TWO BOONS YOU HAD OFFERED ME MANY YEARS AGO? I WANT THEM NOW. IF YOU REFUSE I WILL GIVE UP MY LIFE.

NAME THE BOONS AND I SHALL SEE THAT THEY ARE YOURS.

THEN LET MY SON BE PROCLAIMED HEIR-APPARENT AND LET RAMA BE BANISHED TO THE FOREST FOR FOURTEEN YEARS.

DASHARATHA WAS STUNNED. HAD HE HEARD RIGHT?

NO-O-O-O! I MAY BANISH KAUSALYA OR SUMITRA BUT NEVER RAMA, MY ELDEST SON WHOSE LOVE SUSTAINS MY LIFE.

24

O SINFUL WOMAN, WERE ALL YOUR PRAISES FOR RAMA UTTERED WITH AN ULTERIOR MOTIVE? YOU WILL STAIN THE FAIR NAME OF OUR ROYAL FAMILY WITH THESE BOONS. ASK FOR...

NOTHING STAINS THAT FAIR NAME AS A BROKEN PROMISE; AND A PROMISE TO ONE WHO SAVED THE KING AND THE ROYAL LINE.

SUMITRA WILL NEVER TRUST ME IF I BANISH RAMA. AND KAUSALYA? KAUSALYA, THE PERFECT WIFE, WHOM I HAVE HURT ONLY TO PLEASE YOU.

SO THAT IS IT. THE KINGDOM GOES TO RAMA, ONLY TO PLEASE KAUSALYA. NO! SHE CANNOT BE THE QUEEN MOTHER! RAMA MUST GO!

KAIKEYI, DON'T YOU REMEMBER HOW RAMA HAS ALWAYS LOVED AND WORSHIPPED YOU?

YOUR FUTILE WORDS TIRE ME. WILL YOU KEEP YOUR PROMISE OR WON'T YOU?

RAMA HAS NEVER HURT ANYONE. AM I TO WOUND HIM WITH YOUR PITILESS DEMAND? KAIKEYI, I AM OLD AND MY END IS NEAR. I BEG FOR MERCY.

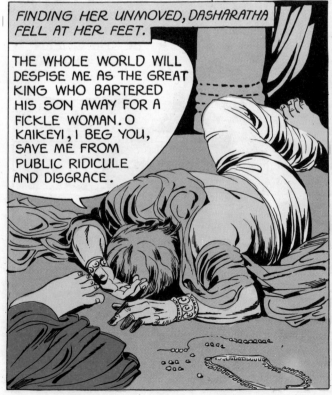

FINDING HER UNMOVED, DASHARATHA FELL AT HER FEET.

THE WHOLE WORLD WILL DESPISE ME AS THE GREAT KING WHO BARTERED HIS SON AWAY FOR A FICKLE WOMAN. O KAIKEYI, I BEG YOU, SAVE ME FROM PUBLIC RIDICULE AND DISGRACE.

BUT KAIKEYI DID NOT RELENT.

O GREAT KING, I SWEAR BY MY OWN BHARATA THAT NOTHING BUT THE EXILE OF RAMA AND THE INSTALLATION OF MY SON, WILL PACIFY ME.

BY THEN, IT WAS ALMOST MORNING.

MY BELOVED SON WILL OBEY ME. OH THAT IT WERE NOT SO! FOR IF HE DOES I WILL DIE. KAIKEYI, I CONSENT. LET RAMA GO TO THE FOREST AND LET THE PREPARATIONS FOR TOMORROW, BE FOR MY FUNERAL.

O KING, DO NOT RAVE LIKE ONE MAD. INSTALL MY SON ON THE THRONE AND BANISH YOURS.

SHOCKED BY HER CRUEL WORDS, DASHARATHA FAINTED. JUST THEN, AN ANXIOUS SUMANTRA SENT BY VASISHTHA CAME THERE.

MY LORD, IT IS TIME FOR THE CEREMONY. WE AWAIT YOUR ORDERS.

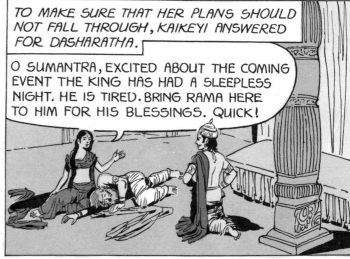

TO MAKE SURE THAT HER PLANS SHOULD NOT FALL THROUGH, KAIKEYI ANSWERED FOR DASHARATHA.

O SUMANTRA, EXCITED ABOUT THE COMING EVENT THE KING HAS HAD A SLEEPLESS NIGHT. HE IS TIRED. BRING RAMA HERE TO HIM FOR HIS BLESSINGS. QUICK!

THE EFFICIENT QUEEN TOO, IS IMPATIENT TO SEE RAMA INSTALLED. I MUST HURRY.

LATER, WHEN THE UNSUSPECTING RAMA PRESENTED HIMSELF BEFORE HIS FATHER—

WHY IS MY FATHER WAN AND DRAINED OF JOY?

MOTHER, HAVE I OFFENDED MY FATHER?

WHEN KAIKEYI TOO PRESENTED A STERN COUNTENANCE—

O MOTHER, HAVE YOU SPOKEN HARSH WORDS TO MY FATHER? WHY DOES HE GRIEVE? TELL ME THE CAUSE, MOTHER. TELL ME THE TRUTH.

THE SHAMELESS KAIKEYI WHOSE HEART HAD BEEN NUMBED BY CUPIDITY, FACED RAMA.

THE KING HOLDS YOU DEARER THAN TRUTH. HE CANNOT COMMAND YOU LEST IT HURT YOU. IF YOU PROMISE TO OBEY HIS WISHES I SHALL SPEAK.

FOR SHAME, MOTHER! WHEN MY FATHER COMMANDS, I OBEY WITHOUT FLINCHING. AND...RAMA NEVER GOES BACK ON HIS WORD.

28

KAIKEYI THEN TOLD RAMA ALL ABOUT THE TWO BOONS. WITHOUT EXPRESSING A TRACE OF DISAPPOINTMENT RAMA FACED KAIKEYI.

YOU ARE MY MOTHER, AND YET KNOW ME NOT. ON YOUR ORDER ALONE I WOULD WILLINGLY SURRENDER NOT ONLY THE KINGDOM BUT ALSO SITA AND MY VERY LIFE.

THERE IS NO GREATER VIRTUE IN THIS WORLD THAN SERVICE TO ONE'S PARENTS IN THOUGHT, WORD AND DEED. SO LET BHARATA RULE THE KINGDOM. AND...

KAIKEYI IMPATIENTLY INTERRUPTED HIS DECLARATIONS.

NOW THAT YOU HAVE TO GO, RAMA, DO NOT DELAY. I SHALL HAVE BHARATA BROUGHT IMMEDIATELY.

AND I SHALL GO AND TAKE LEAVE OF MY MOTHER AND OFFER MY CONSOLATION TO SITA.

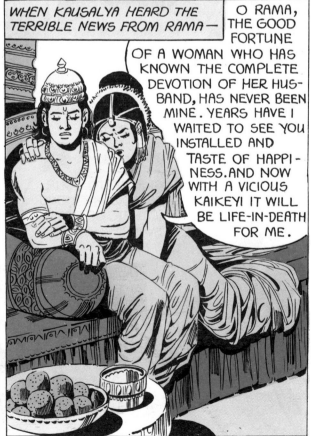

WHEN KAUSALYA HEARD THE TERRIBLE NEWS FROM RAMA—

O RAMA, THE GOOD FORTUNE OF A WOMAN WHO HAS KNOWN THE COMPLETE DEVOTION OF HER HUSBAND, HAS NEVER BEEN MINE. YEARS HAVE I WAITED TO SEE YOU INSTALLED AND TASTE OF HAPPINESS. AND NOW WITH A VICIOUS KAIKEYI IT WILL BE LIFE-IN-DEATH FOR ME.

RAMA DID NOT TRY TO CONSOLE HIS MOTHER. INSTEAD —

MOTHER, MY FATHER'S COMMAND BINDS US BOTH.

YES, MY WORTHY SON. MAY YOU BE HAPPY IN EXILE. I SHALL SERVE YOUR FATHER DUTIFULLY WHILE I PRAY FOR YOUR SAFE RETURN.

AS RAMA LEFT FOR THE FOREST, WITH LAKSHMANA AND SITA WHO INSISTED ON GOING WITH HIM, DASHARATHA COLLAPSED WITH GRIEF. KAIKEYI REACHED OUT TO HELP HIM.

KEEP AWAY, O VILE KAIKEYI, YOUR TOUCH WILL POLLUTE ME. YOU WILL ENJOY YOUR BOONS BUT AS A WIDOW. FOR I WILL NOT LIVE LONG WITHOUT RAMA.

THEN HE TURNED TO KAUSALYA.

TAKE ME TO YOUR PALACE, O VIRTUOUS MOTHER OF RAMA. NOWHERE ELSE WILL I KNOW PEACE.

ON THE FIFTH DAY AFTER RAMA LEFT, KAUSALYA, UNABLE TO RESTRAIN HERSELF ANY LONGER, TURNED UPON THE KING.

O KING, IGNORING ME YOU BANISHED MY SON. I MAY NOT EVEN FOLLOW HIM LEST YOU BE DESOLATE. YOU HAVE RUINED ME AND MY SON AND ALL AYODHYA.

FULL OF ANGUISH, DASHARATHA PLEADED WITH HER.

PLEASE, KAUSALYA, I ENTREAT YOU, I AM YOUR HUSBAND, VIRTUOUS OR WORTHLESS. AND I KNOW YOU TO BE WISE.

KAUSALYA, MOVED BY THE GREAT MONARCH'S HUMILITY, WAS ASHAMED OF HER OWN OUTBURST.

O LORD, DO NOT SHAME ME. A WELL-BRED WOMAN SHOULD NEVER MAKE A SUPPLICANT OF HER LORD. PARDON MY TRANSGRESSION.

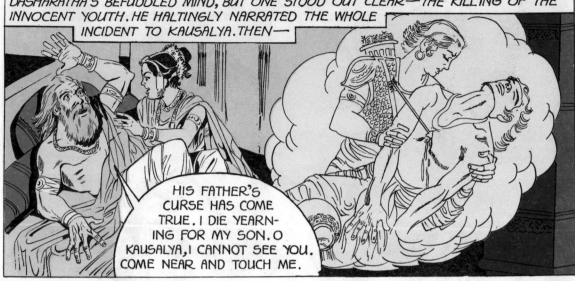

ON THE SIXTH NIGHT OF RAMA'S DEPARTURE, A MEDLEY OF PAST DEEDS RACED ACROSS DASHARATHA'S BEFUDDLED MIND, BUT ONE STOOD OUT CLEAR—THE KILLING OF THE INNOCENT YOUTH. HE HALTINGLY NARRATED THE WHOLE INCIDENT TO KAUSALYA. THEN—

HIS FATHER'S CURSE HAS COME TRUE. I DIE YEARNING FOR MY SON. O KAUSALYA, I CANNOT SEE YOU. COME NEAR AND TOUCH ME.

SEEING THAT HIS END WAS NEAR, KAUSALYA SENT FOR SUMITRA.

O MY PRINCE, MY SON, WHERE ARE YOU? O KAUSALYA! AH, GENTLE SUMITRA! I...

NO! LORD DO NOT LEAVE US AND GO...

OVERCOME BY GRIEF FOR HIS EXILED SON, DASHARATHA, A VICTIM OF HIS OWN KARMA, BREATHED HIS LAST.

BUT ALL KAIKEYI'S EFFORTS TO SECURE THE THRONE FOR HER SON WERE FUTILE. FOR BHARATA WOULD NOT ASCEND IT. WHEN RAMA REFUSED TO RETURN TO AYODHYA TILL HE HAD FULFILLED HIS PLEDGE, BHARATA PLACED RAMA'S SLIPPERS ON THE THRONE AND RULED THE KINGDOM FOR HIM, TILL HE RETURNED TO BE THE KING.

Rama

AMAR CHITRA KATHA

Illustrated Classics From India

Rama

Ramayana is the earliest epic poem written in Sanskrit, is the oldest work of genuine poetry. In that sense its author, sage Valmiki is known as the 'Adi Kavi' or pristine poet.

It is said that the poem flowed from the compassionate heart of Valmiki when he witnessed the sorrow of a female Krauncha bird when the merciless arrow of a hunter killed its mate. This 'spontaneous overflow of powerful emotions' saw the evolution of a powerful epic that still inspires the soul of India – 2000 years since its creation.

Ramayana is an integral part of our heritage such that our apparent diversities are reflected in slightly differing versions written in various languages. The Ramayanas of Kamban, Tulsidas, Kirtivas and Tunchan, are variations of the same theme.

This sublime theme is embodied in the character of Rama and Sita – the highest ideals of 'man' and 'woman'. The idea that God fulfils Himself in the best of men is conveyed through Rama's life. This is the story of Ramayana.

The story narrated in the following pages is based on Ramcharit-Manas of Tulsidas.

Illustrations : Pratap Mulick   Cover : Pratap Mulick

RAMA

ON THE BANK OF THE RIVER SARAYU STANDS THE CITY OF AYODHYA. LONG AGO, RAJA DASHARATHA RULED OVER IT. HE HAD FOUR SONS- RAMA, LAXMANA, BHARATA AND SHATRUGHNA.

RAMA WAS BORN OF QUEEN KAUSHALYA, BHARATA OF QUEEN KAIKEYI AND LAXMANA AND SHATRUGHNA OF QUEEN SUMITRA. BUT THEY WERE ALL DEEPLY ATTACHED TO ONE ANOTHER.

RAMA'S SKILL WITH THE BOW AND ARROW WAS KNOWN FAR AND WIDE. IN THE JUNGLE, SAGE VISHWAMITRA ALSO REMEMBERED IT.

SO, WITH THE PERMISSION OF KING DASHARATHA, RAMA AND LAXMANA WERE BROUGHT TO THE JUNGLE. ONE DAY—

RAMA! HERE COMES THE DEMONESS TATAKA.

THERE WAS A FIERCE BATTLE BETWEEN TATAKA AND RAMA.

AND FINALLY—

THERE WERE MORE RAIDS BY DEMONS. BUT RAMA'S ARROWS NEVER MISSED THEIR MARK.

ONE AFTER ANOTHER, PRINCES TRIED TO STRING THE BOW. THEY COULD NOT EVEN LIFT IT.

EACH ONE OF US HAS FAILED. SURELY WE CAN LIFT THIS BOW TOGETHER!

RAMA, MY SON! ALL THE OTHERS HAVE FAILED. NOW LIFT THE BOW AND BRING HAPPINESS TO SITA!

RAMA LIFTED THE BOW EASILY. IT BROKE UNDER HIS STRENGTH.

SITA LOOKED UP AND WAS PLEASED TO SEE RAMA.

WHEN THE HAPPY NEWS REACHED AYODHYA, KING DASHARATHA LEFT FOR MITHILA, AT THE HEAD OF A PROCESSION..

... WHERE RAMA WAS MARRIED TO SITA.

SO WHAT?

QUEEN KAUSHALYA'S SON WILL RULE. AND YOU WILL HAVE TO SERVE BOTH THE MOTHER AND SON!

THE WICKED MAID'S WORDS HAD THEIR EFFECT ON KAIKEYI.

THE KING ONCE PROMISED TO GRANT YOU TWO WISHES. MAKE THEM NOW—LET BHARATA BE CROWNED KING AND LET RAMA BE SENT INTO EXILE FOR FOURTEEN YEARS.

LATER—

WHY THIS DISPLEASURE MY DEAR?

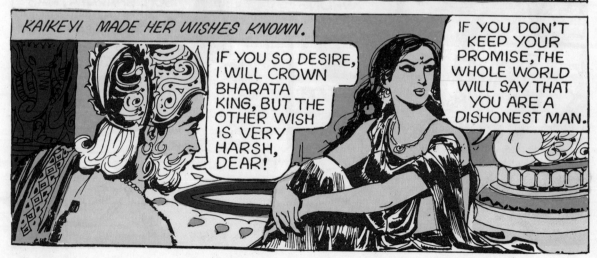

KAIKEYI MADE HER WISHES KNOWN.

IF YOU SO DESIRE, I WILL CROWN BHARATA KING, BUT THE OTHER WISH IS VERY HARSH, DEAR!

IF YOU DON'T KEEP YOUR PROMISE, THE WHOLE WORLD WILL SAY THAT YOU ARE A DISHONEST MAN.

THE KING FELL DOWN ON THE GROUND WHEN HE HEARD THESE HARSH WORDS.

HOW COULD YOU BE SO CRUEL TO RAMA? HE IS SO GOOD AND NOBLE.

WHEN RAMA LEARNT OF IT —

I SHALL KEEP MY FATHER'S PROMISE, MOTHER!

SITA AND LAXMANA ALSO INSISTED ON ACCOMPANYING RAMA TO THE JUNGLES. THE PEOPLE OF AYODHYA ALSO FOLLOWED THEM.

MINISTER, SIR, COULDN'T YOU PERSUADE THESE PEOPLE TO GO BACK?

WE SHALL ALL COME WITH YOU.

WHEN DUSK FELL, THEY STOPPED AND RESTED. EARLY NEXT MORNING—

LET US BE GONE BEFORE THE PEOPLE WAKE UP AND INSIST ON GOING WITH US.

NEAR THE BANK OF THE RIVER GANGA, RAMA, LAXMANA AND SITA TOOK LEAVE OF THE MINISTER

SIR, HENCEFORTH OUR WAYS ARE DIFFERENT. WE GO SOUTH ACROSS THE RIVER. YOU GO BACK TO AYODHYA.

BACK IN AYODHYA, THE MINISTER PRESENTED HIMSELF BEFORE THE KING.

O-OH! RAMA!

AND DASHARATHA DIED REMEMBERING HIS SON RAMA.

BACK FROM HIS VISIT TO HIS UNCLE'S, BHARATA WENT STRAIGHT TO HIS MOTHER.

WHAT'S WRONG, MOTHER? EVERYTHING IS SO QUIET HERE.

EVERYTHING IS FINE-AT LEAST FOR YOU. NOW, YOU WILL BE THE KING. YOUR FATHER IS DEAD AND RAMA HAS GONE AWAY TO THE JUNGLES FOR FOURTEEN YEARS.

BHARATA WAS SHOCKED TO HEAR THE DETAILS. VASI-SHTHA, THE ROYAL PRIEST, TRIED TO CONSOLE HIM.

I DON'T WANT THE KINGDOM. I MUST GO TO RAMA AT ONCE.

FORGET YOUR SORROW! ATTEND TO THE MATTERS OF STATE! THAT IS YOUR DUTY!

AT CHITRAKOOT, WHERE RAMA, LAXMANA AND SITA HAD MADE THEIR HOME—

BHARATA IS MARCHING HIS ARMIES AGAINST US. I WILL...

LAXMANA, DON'T BE SO HASTY. LET THEM COME!

BHARATA, MY DEAR BROTHER!

DEAR RAMA! WE ALL WANT YOU TO GO BACK TO AYODHYA!

FORGIVE ME GURUDEV, I CAN'T BREAK MY FATHER'S PROMISE.

AND I CAN NOT ACCEPT THE KINGDOM. IF YOU ARE NOT COMING BACK, I SHALL RULE IN YOUR NAME. YOUR SANDALS WILL REPRESENT YOU.

AFTER BHARATA LEFT, RAMA, LAXMANA AND SITA SETTLED DOWN IN PANCHAVATI TOWN IN THE SOUTH. ONE DAY—

A HANDSOME MAN! AND POWERFUL TOO! I MUST WIN HIS LOVE.

NOBLE SIR, SHOORPANAKHA IS MY NAME. I OFFER MY LOVE; DO ACCEPT IT.

I AM A HAPPILY MARRIED MAN, LADY! YOU COULD ASK LAXMANA!

I AM ONLY HIS SERVANT! HE IS THE ONE FOR YOU.

SHOORPANAKHA ASSUMED A FRIGHTENING FORM AND RUSHED TOWARDS SITA.

ENRAGED, LAXMANA CHOPPED OFF HER NOSE AND EARS. SHE RAN TO HER COUSINS, KHARA AND DOOSHANA, FOR HELP.

OH-OH! KHAR! DOOSHAN!

KHAR! DOOSHAN! THEY DARED TO DO THIS TO YOUR SISTER!

WE WILL FIGHT THEM, SISTER!

KHARA AND DOOSHANA CAME WITH A MIGHTY ARMY OF DEMONS TO FIGHT RAMA.

THEY HAVE KILLED BOTH KHARA AND DOOSHANA! RUN FOR YOUR LIVES!

THE TEN-HEADED RAVANA, THE KING OF LANKA, WAS THE BROTHER OF SHOORPANAKHA. SHE NOW APPROACHED HIM.

YOU WILL BE AVENGED, MY SISTER! FIRST LET ME CONSULT UNCLE MAREECHA!

RAVANA! RAMA IS POWERFUL. TO FIGHT HIM IS NOT EASY.

YOU ASSUME THE FORM OF A GOLDEN DEER AND LURE RAMA AWAY. MEANWHILE I WILL RUN AWAY WITH SITA.

RAVANA APPROACHED MAREECHA.

THAT DEER IS SO BEAUTIFUL! I WANT IT.

I WILL GET IT FOR YOU, SITA.

IN PANCHAVATI —

RAMA CHASED THE DEER DEEP INTO THE JUNGLE — THE DEER CRIED OUT LOUDLY IN A HUMAN VOICE.

OH! LAXMANA!

RAMA IS CALLING YOU, LAXMANA.

BUT RAMA HAS ASKED ME NOT TO LEAVE YOU ALONE.

YOU MUST GO TO HELP YOUR BROTHER. LAXMANA.

I DIDN'T CALL YOU, LAXMANA! IT WAS A TRICK PLAYED BY THIS DEMON.

MEANWHILE, DISGUISED AS A SANYASI, RAVANA APPROACHED SITA.

WILL THE KIND LADY OFFER ME SOME FOOD?

AS SITA BROUGHT HIM FOOD, RAVANA CAUGHT HOLD OF HER...

...AND CARRIED HER AWAY IN HIS CHARIOT.

HELP! RAMA! LAXMANA! HELP!

SOMEONE SAVE ME FROM THIS DEVIL! PLEASE!

JATAYU, THE VULTURE, CAME TO HER HELP.

YOU OLD FOOL! YOU DARED TO FIGHT RAVANA!

WHEN RAMA REACHED THE SPOT IN SEARCH OF SITA —

I FAILED TO RESCUE SITA. RAVANA HAS TAKEN HER TO THE SOUTH.

POOR JATAYU HE GAVE HIS LIFE FOR ME!

TRAVELLING FURTHER SOUTH, RAMA MET SUGREEVA, BROTHER OF THE MONKEY KING VALI AND HIS MINISTER HANUMAN.

I AM ALSO SAD, RAMA. I LIVE IN THE JUNGLE FOR FEAR OF VALI, MY BROTHER, WHO HAS KIDNAPPED MY WIFE. HELP ME TO OVERTHROW VALI AND I WILL HELP YOU.

RAMA KILLED VALI AND SET SUGREEVA ON THE THRONE. VALI'S SON, ANGADA. WAS CROWNED PRINCE.

LATER —

NOW HANUMAN! YOU MUST GO IN SEARCH OF SITA.

HERE, HANUMAN! TAKE THIS RING. IF YOU FIND SITA, SHE WILL RECOGNISE THIS.

HANUMAN DROPPED RAMA'S RING.

I CAN'T LIVE WITHOUT RAMA. I WOULD RATHER KILL MYSELF... RAMA'S RING! HOW DID IT GET HERE!

I BROUGHT THIS RING WITH ME. I WILL TELL HIM YOU ARE HERE AND HE WILL SURELY COME AND KILL RAVANA!

HANUMAN JUMPED DOWN.

BUT BEFORE I GO, I MUST TEACH THESE DEMONS A LESSON.

IT IS THAT MONKEY! GET HIM! GET HIM!

HANUMAN HAD KNOCKED DOWN THE DEMONS IN AND AROUND THE GARDEN. RAVANA SENT MORE MEN WITH HIS SON, AKSHAYA KUMAR.

IN RAVANA'S COURT —

NOW, MEGHNAD, MY SON, ARREST THAT MONKEY AND BRING HIM HERE!

THAT MONKEY HAS KILLED PRINCE AKSHAY KUMAR AS WELL!

MEGHNAD CAPTURED HANUMAN AND BROUGHT HIM TO THE COURT.

SET FIRE TO THIS EVIL MONKEY'S TAIL.

THIS WILL BE FUN TO WATCH.

HANUMAN LOOSENED THE ROPES THAT BOUND HIM. HIS TAIL GREW BIGGER AND BIGGER. WITH HIS LONG TAIL AFIRE, HE SET FIRE TO THE WHOLE OF LANKA.

RUN! RUN FOR YOUR LIVES! THIS MONKEY IS DANGEROUS.

HAVING BURNT LANKA, HANUMAN RETURNED TO RAMA'S CAMP.

SITA IS IN LANKA. SHE ASKED ME TO GIVE YOU THIS JEWEL. LANKA SHOULD NOW BE INVADED!

WITH A HUGE ARMY OF MONKEYS, BEARS AND OTHERS, RAMA, LAXMANA, SUGREEVA AND HANUMAN ARRIVED ON THE COAST.

WHEN THE NEWS REACHED THE COURT OF RAVANA, HIS BROTHER, VIBHEESHANA GAVE HIM GOOD ADVICE.

ABDUCTING ANOTHER MAN'S WIFE IS NEITHER FAIR NOR WISE!

GET OUT OF HERE, VIBHEESHANA. GO, TEACH YOUR WISDOM TO THOSE BEGGARS!

NOBLE RAMA GAVE REFUGE TO VIBHEESHANA.

THE ENEMY'S BROTHER — IN OUR CAMP? I DON'T LIKE THE IDEA!

HE SEEKS ASYLUM, SUGREEVA! I CAN'T TURN HIM AWAY.

A BRIDGE WAS LAID ACROSS THE SEA.

TO LANKA

TO LANKA

TO LANKA

THE ARMIES WERE READY FOR THE BATTLE.

ANGADA, BEFORE WE GIVE THE CALL FOR BATTLE, PLEASE GO TO RAVANA'S COURT WITH A MESSAGE.

PRINCE ANGADA CAME TO THE COURT OF RAVANA.

RETURN SITA WITH HONOUR. LORD RAMA WILL MAKE PEACE WITH YOU.

GO, TELL RAMA THAT I WILL NOT SURRENDER! WE WANT WAR!

ANGADA RETURNED AND THE BATTLE CALL WAS GIVEN.

BRAVE LAXMANA FELL IN THE BATTLE, HIT WITH AN ARROW BY MEGHNAD, RAVANA'S SON.

IF ONLY THE PHYSICIAN SUSHENA COULD BE BROUGHT HERE...

I WILL BRING HIM!

HANUMAN BROUGHT SUSHENA ALONG WITH HIS HOUSE.

LAXMANA CAN BE BROUGHT BACK TO LIFE IF SOMEONE CAN GET THE SANJEE-VANI HERB BEFORE DAWN.

I WILL GET IT.

RAMA WAS HEART-BROKEN.

WITHOUT YOU, BROTHER, I HAVE NO DESIRE TO LIVE!

HERE IS THE HILL-SANJEEVANI AND ALL.

THE SANJEEVANI HERB WORKED QUICKLY. LAXMANA SAT UP AND EVERYONE WAS HAPPY.

BUT NOW RAVANA'S BROTHER KUMBHA-KARNA STARTED PLAYING HAVOC ON THE MONKEY ARMY.

HOWEVER, RAMA WAS MORE THAN A MATCH FOR HIM.

AND SOON KUMBHAKARNA FELL.

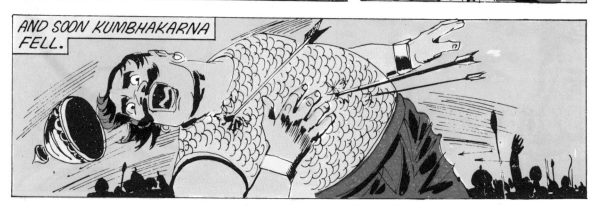

RAVANA'S SON MEGHNAD WAS KILLED BY LAXMANA.

THE DEMONS WERE NOW ON THE RUN.

IN RAVANA'S CAMP—

HAVE THEY KILLED MEGHNAD?

DETERMINED TO KILL RAMA, RAVANA FOUGHT HARD.

HE SHOWERED A CONTINUOUS STREAM OF ARROWS WITH HIS TWENTY HANDS ON THE MONKEY ARMY.

LAXMANA! MURDERER OF MY SON! YOU WILL NOT LIVE!

THEN RAMA AND RAVANA CAME FACE TO FACE. NOW RAMA HAD A CHARIOT SENT TO HIM BY GOD INDRA.

YOU CAN'T FIGHT RAVANA AND LIVE! THIS BORROWED CHARIOT WILL NOT SAVE YOU!

WITH HIS SUPERNATURAL POWERS, RAVANA CREATED SEVERAL RAVANAS.

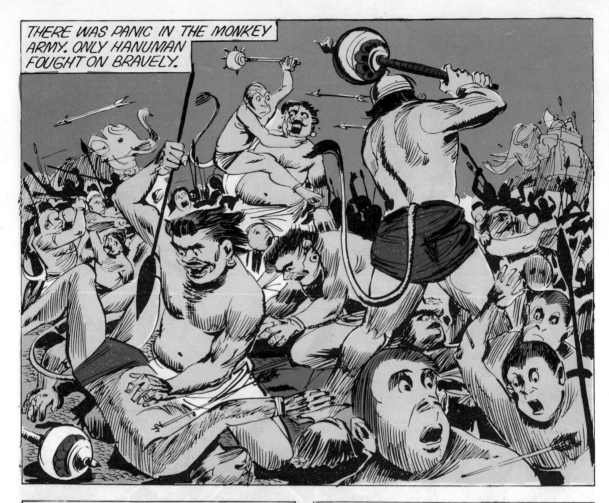

THERE WAS PANIC IN THE MONKEY ARMY. ONLY HANUMAN FOUGHT ON BRAVELY.

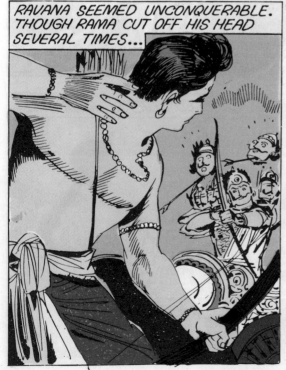

RAVANA SEEMED UNCONQUERABLE. THOUGH RAMA CUT OFF HIS HEAD SEVERAL TIMES...

...ANOTHER TOOK ITS PLACE AS SOON AS ONE HEAD ROLLED OFF.

VIBHEESHANA, DURING THE PAST EIGHTEEN DAYS, I HAVE CUT OFF RAVANA'S HEAD A NUMBER OF TIMES. BUT HE CONTINUES TO LIVE.

HE DOES SO BECAUSE THE NECTAR OF LIFE IS STORED IN HIS NAVEL!

RAMA SHOT ONE ARROW AT THE NAVEL OF RAVANA! SOON ALL HIS HEADS AND ARMS WERE STRUCK WITH ARROWS.

RAVANA FELL.

GLORY TO PRINCE RAMA.

VIBHEESHANA! NOW YOU WILL RULE OVER LANKA!

LAXMANA CROWNED HIM CEREMONIOUSLY.

AFTER CROWNING VIBHEE-SHANA, RAMA LEFT FOR AYODHYA IN THE PUSHPAK AIRCRAFT.

SITA, MY DEAR, YOUR DAYS OF UNHAPPINESS ARE NOW OVER!

RAMA WAS CROWNED KING IN AYODHYA AND HE RULED FOR MANY YEARS.

Hanuman

Illustrated Classics From India

Hanuman

Hanuman, the son of Anjana and the Wind God, Pavana or Vayu, was born a monkey. Yet, he occupies a prominent place among the Hindu gods for his sterling character. Hanuman is renowned for his strength and valour besides his steadfast love and loyalty to Lord Rama. He is the embodiment of devotion and power. Hanuman's unflinching devotion to Rama has made him one of the greatest bhaktas (devotees) ever known. In fact, Hanuman is often referred to as Ramabhakta Hanuman. His singular worship of Rama made him compassionate. It helped him leap across 800 miles of ocean to Lanka and console Sita who was pining for Rama, forlorn and lonely in Ravana's Ashoka garden.

Hanuman was the chief general of the monkey king, Sugreeva. The story of his adventures, particularly after the monkey army reaches the seashore opposite Lanka, is one of the best efforts of pure imagination to be found in the Ramayana. Years later, this virtue also helped Hanuman submit himself to the buoyant valour of Rama's children , Luv and Kush.

Script: Anant Pai   Illustrations: Ram Waeerkar   Cover : Ram Waeerkar

AS HE GREW, HIS STRENGTH GREW WITH HIM. ONE DAY, WITH HIS BARE HANDS, HE SAVED PRINCE SUGREEVA, FROM THE CHARGE OF A WILD ELEPHANT.

THANKS FOR YOUR TIMELY HELP, HANUMAN!

PRINCE SUGREEVA, I'M HONOURED!

WHEN VALI, THE KING OF KISH-KINDHA BANISHED HIS BROTHER, SUGREEVA, FROM HIS KINGDOM, HANUMAN WENT WITH HIM TO THE JUNGLES NEAR THE RIVER PAMPA. THERE THEY LIVED A HARD LIFE.

ONE DAY—

THERE ARE TWO MEN COMING THIS WAY.

HAVE THEY COME FROM VALI? HANUMAN! PLEASE GO AND FIND OUT WHO THEY ARE.

HANUMAN ASSUMED THE FORM OF A POOR MAN AND APPROACHED THE STRANGERS.

WHERE ARE YOU ASCETICS GOING, SIR?

WE ARE LOOKING FOR SUGREEVA, THE VANARA KING.

THIS IS MY ELDER BROTHER RAMA, THE BANISHED PRINCE OF AYODHYA. HIS WIFE SITA WAS ABDUCTED BY RAVANA, THE DEMON KING. WE WANT SUGREEVA TO HELP US FIND SITA.

LISTENING TO LAXMANA, HANUMAN'S HEART WAS SUDDENLY FILLED WITH A STRANGE FEELING OF LOVE AND ADORATION.

HANUMAN THREW AWAY HIS DISGUISE AND FELL PROSTRATE AT RAMA'S FEET.

FORGIVE ME, I'M REALLY HANUMAN, SUGREEVA'S MINISTER.

WILL YOU TAKE US TO SUGREEVA?

HANUMAN JOYFULLY CARRIED RAMA AND LAXMANA ON HIS SHOULDERS.

IT WAS A HAPPY MEETING. THE TWO BROTHERS KNEW, THEY HAD FOUND FRIENDS.

WHY DO YOU WANT TO KILL YOUR BROTHER?

WILL YOU HELP ME KILL VALI?

"ONCE VALI AND I HAD GONE TO FIGHT A DEMON. THERE WAS A BIG CAVE. VALI ASKED ME TO WAIT OUTSIDE AND WENT IN. WHEN HE DID NOT COME OUT FOR A LONG TIME, I THOUGHT HE WAS DEAD AND CAME BACK.

"THE THRONE COULD NOT REMAIN VACANT. THE PEOPLE CROWNED ME AS KING. THEN ONE DAY VALI CAME BACK..."

"...AND DROVE ME AWAY."

SINCE THEN I HAVE BEEN RUNNING FROM HIM. WILL YOU HELP ME TO KILL HIM?

YES, I WILL!

SUGREEVA BROUGHT A SMALL BUNDLE TO RAMA.

WE SAW A LADY BEING CARRIED AWAY IN RAVANA'S CHARIOT. SHE THREW THESE DOWN TO US.

YES, THESE ARE SITA'S JEWELS.

SUGREEVA CALLED VALI TO A DUEL. RAMA WAITED FOR A CHANCE TO KILL VALI. BUT HE COULD NOT RECOGNISE HIM. BOTH THE BROTHERS LOOKED ALIKE.

FOR THE NEXT ROUND, RAMA GAVE SUGREEVA A GARLAND TO WEAR. THIS TIME HIS ARROW FOUND ITS MARK.

SUGREEVA WAS CROWNED THE KING OF KISH-KINDHA. VALI'S SON ANGADA BECAME THE CROWN PRINCE.

LONG LIVE KING SUGREEVA!

LONG LIVE PRINCE ANGADA!

SUGREEVA SENT HIS BRAVE MONKEYS TO SEARCH SITA IN THE FOUR CORNERS OF THE WORLD.

WE MUST LOOK EVERYWHERE!

WE MUST FIND HER!

THE MONKEYS WENT OUT IN DIFFERENT DIRECTIONS.

HANUMAN, ANGADA AND JAMBA-VAAN WENT SOUTH, UNTIL THEY CAME TO THE OCEAN.

ON A HILL NEARBY THEY MET THE VULTURE KING.

ACROSS THE OCEAN LIES LANKA-RAVANA'S CAPITAL CITY. SITA IS A PRISONER THERE.

ACROSS THE SEA? A DISTANCE OF HUNDRED YOJANAS? HOW CAN WE CROSS THE SEA?

I CAN JUMP TWENTY YOJANAS!

I CAN DO THIRTY!

YOU JAMBA-VAAN?

HOW FAR CAN YOU GO?

I'M OLD, YET I CAN MANAGE NINETY, MAYBE!

WHILE THE DISCUSSION WENT ON, HANUMAN SAT QUIETLY. NOW ALL TURNED TO HIM.

HANUMAN, YOU ARE THE ONLY ONE WHO CAN MAKE THIS TRIP. WILL YOU GO?

CERTAINLY!

LIKE A GREAT BIRD, HANUMAN LEAPED INTO THE SKY.

A GIANT MOUNTAIN SUDDENLY ROSE FROM THE OCEAN AND BLOCKED HANUMAN'S WAY. HANUMAN STRUCK THE MOUNTAIN WITH HIS CHEST.

I AM MAINAKA. YOUR FATHER HAD ONCE SAVED MY LIFE. YOU MUST WAIT FOR A WHILE!

THANK YOU! BUT I CANNOT WAIT!

AS HANUMAN WENT FLYING, SURASA, THE SEA MONSTER CAME OUT WITH HER JAWS WIDE OPEN.

YOU MUST ENTER MY MOUTH!

HANUMAN STARTED BLOWING HIM- SELF UP BIGGER AND BIGGER...

...AND THE MONSTER OPENED HER JAWS WIDER AND WIDER.

SUDDENLY HANUMAN BECAME VERY SMALL AND BEFORE THE MONSTER COULD REALISE IT, HE ENTERED HER MOUTH AND CAME OUT AGAIN.

YOUR WISH IS FULFILLED. I DID ENTER YOUR MOUTH.

YOU ARE BRAVE. I WAS ONLY TESTING YOUR DETERMINATION.

AT LAST HANUMAN REACHED THE SHORES OF LANKA.

HOW SHALL I ENTER THE CITY? THERE ARE GUARDS ALL AROUND. LET ME BECOME SMALL. NOBODY WILL NOTICE ME.

HANUMAN ROAMED THE CITY FROM STREET TO STREET, FROM HOUSE TO HOUSE...

...THERE WERE MIGHTY WAR ELEPHANTS...

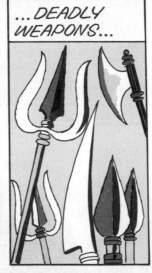

...DEADLY WEAPONS...

...AND GIANT WARRIORS GUARDING THE WALLS.

LANKA WAS A DAZZLING, BEAUTIFUL CITY. BUT HANUMAN WAS SOMEWHAT SAD.

ALL THIS WILL BE DESTROYED WHEN MY MASTER COMES TO FIGHT RAVANA.

AFTER SURVEYING THE CITY, HANUMAN WENT INTO RAVANA'S PALACE.

IT WAS NIGHT. THE WHOLE PALACE WAS ASLEEP...

...THERE WERE THE BEAUTIFUL QUEENS...

THERE WAS INDRAJIT—RAVANA'S WARRIOR SON.

AND KUMBHAKARNA, RAVANA'S BROTHER, WHO SLEPT SIX MONTHS OF THE YEAR.

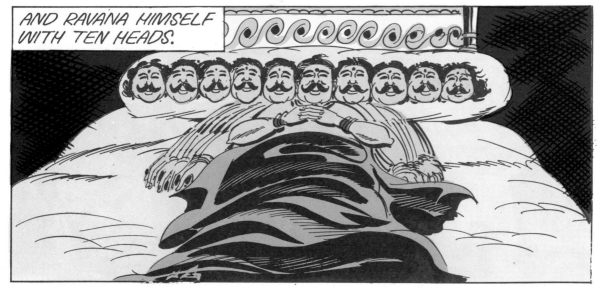

AND RAVANA HIMSELF WITH TEN HEADS.

IN RAVANA'S CHAMBER, HANUMAN SAW A BEAUTIFUL WOMAN ASLEEP.

IS SHE SITA? NO, NEVER! HOW COULD I THINK SHE WOULD GIVE HERSELF TO THIS BRUTE?

NOT FINDING SITA IN THE PALACE, HANUMAN WENT TO THE ASHOKA GARDEN ADJOINING THE PALACE.

UNDER A TREE SAT SITA, SLEEPLESS, THINKING OF RAMA.

I CAN'T APPROACH HER! SHE IS SURROUNDED BY DEMONS.

HANUMAN REMAINED HIDDEN IN A TREE. IN THE DAWN CAME RAVANA.

ARE YOU STILL DETERMINED NOT TO BE MY WIFE?

IT'S WRONO TO TALK LIKE THAT.

I CAN HEAR THE TWANG OF MY HUSBAND'S BOW. YOUR DAYS ARE NUMBERED.

HA! WHAT CAN RAMA DO?

AFTER RAVANA HAD GONE, THE RAKSHASIS BEGAN TEASING SITA.

MARRY HIM! WHERE ELSE CAN YOU GET SUCH A HUSBAND?

HOW MUCH MORE CAN I ENDURE?

WHEN SITA WAS LEFT ALONE FOR SOME TIME, HANUMAN TOOK OUT THE SIGNET RING RAMA HAD GIVEN HIM AND DROPPED IT ON HER LAP.

WHAT IS THIS? MY HUSBAND'S RING?

HANUMAN CLIMBED DOWN FROM THE TREE AND STOOD IN FRONT OF SITA. HE RELATED EVERYTHING TO HER.

MY MASTER WILL SOON COME TO SAVE YOU!

I CAN CARRY YOU ON MY BACK. PLEASE COME WITH ME.

NO! FOR HIS HONOUR HE MUST COME AND FIGHT RAVANA. HERE, TAKE THIS JEWEL TO HIM. HE WILL KNOW.

HANUMAN DECIDED TO TEACH RAVANA A LESSON.

HOW DO YOU LIKE THAT?

THAT GOES FOR YOU!

UPROOTING TREES, BEATING RAKSHASAS, HANUMAN CREATED HAVOC IN RAVANA'S PALACE.

HELP!

IS HE A DEMON?

RUN FOR YOUR LIVES!

THE PANIC-STRICKEN RAKSHASAS RUSHED TO RAVANA.

A MONSTER HAS ENTERED THE GARDEN, YOUR MAJESTY!

RAVANA SENT HIS SOLDIERS TO CAPTURE HANUMAN. BUT NO ONE COULD COME NEAR HIM.

THEN CAME INDRA-JIT, RAVANA'S WARRIOR SON.

INDRAJIT COULD NOT SUBDUE HANUMAN WHO HAD BY NOW ASSUMED HIS NORMAL SIZE. THEN HE USED HIS MIGHTIEST WEAPON, THE SNAKE ARROWS. HANUMAN LAY MOTIONLESS, TIED BY THE COILS.

THE RAKSHASAS BOUND HIM TIGHTLY.

I SHALL NOT FREE MYSELF! THIS IS THE ONLY WAY I CAN ENTER RAVANA'S COURT.

HANUMAN WAS CARRIED INTO THE DAZZLING THRONE ROOM.

CALL THE EXECUTIONER!

VIBHEESHANA, RAVANA'S RIGHTEOUS BROTHER INTERVENED.

YOU CANNOT KILL A MESSENGER!

THE RAKSHASAS TIED PIECES OF CLOTH AROUND HANUMAN'S TAIL AND POURED OIL. BUT THE TAIL GREW...

...LONGER

BRING MORE CLOTH!

MORE OIL!

...AND STILL LONGER.

THERE IS NO MORE OIL.

TELL THE KING!

BUT HANUMAN'S TAIL KEPT GROWING.

THE PALACE HAS NO MORE OIL!

WHAT IS THE MATTER NOW?

ALL RIGHT! LIGHT THE FLAME!

THE SOLDIERS TOOK HIM THROUGH THE STREETS.

FOOLS! THEY ARE SHOWING ME THE WHOLE PLAN OF THE CITY!

SUDDENLY HANUMAN SHRANK HIS SIZE. THE ROPES SLIPPED DOWN TO THE GROUND.

WITH A MIGHTY ROAR HE LEAPT TO A HOUSE TOP.

LONG LIVE RAMA! LONG LIVE SITA!

HANUMAN LEAPED FROM ONE HOUSETOP TO ANOTHER SETTING FIRE TO THE CITY.

HANUMAN WENT TO THE SEA TO EXTINGUISH HIS TAIL. HIS MISSION WAS MORE THAN COMPLETE.

ON THE OTHER STORE, THE VANARAS PATIENTLY AWAITED HIS RETURN.

THERE HE COMES!

IN THEIR JOY, THE VANARAS LIFTED HANUMAN ABOVE THEIR HEADS AND DANCED AROUND.

LONG LIVE HANUMAN!

THE SEARCH PARTY AT LAST RETURNED HOME.

SITA'S CROWN JEWEL!

MY DEAREST WIFE!

SUGREEVA ORDERED THE ARMY TO ASSEMBLE...

THE GREAT MONKEY ARMY FELL IN LINE...

...AND THE GIANT BEARS TOO!

THE GREAT ARMY REACHED THE SEASHORE. ON THE OTHER SIDE LAY LANKA WHERE SITA WAS A PRISONER.

HOW CAN WE CROSS THE MIGHTY OCEAN?

A BRIDGE? HOW?

NALA IS A GREAT ENGINEER MONKEY! HE CAN BUILD A BRIDGE!

CAN'T WE BUILD A BRIDGE?

MEANWHILE, VIBHEESHANA, RAVANA'S BROTHER HAD COME OVER TO JOIN RAMA.

I DO NOT WISH TO LIVE WITH MY SINFUL BROTHER WILL YOU GIVE ME SHELTER?

HOW CAN WE TRUST HIM?

THIS MAY BE A TRICK!

I THINK WE CAN BELIEVE HIM. HOWEVER, EVEN IF IT BE A TRICK, I CANNOT TURN AWAY SOMEONE WHO ASKS FOR SHELTER!

SOON NALA STARTED BUILDING A BRIDGE OF STONES.

THE HUGE STONES WERE RE-LAYED FROM HAND TO HAND DOWN THE MOUNTAINS...

...AND THE BRIDGE WAS READY.

THE ARMY STARTED OUT ON ITS MARCH.

HANUMAN CARRIED RAMA ON HIS SHOULDERS. ANGADA CARRIED LAXMANA.

THE OCEAN WAS CROSSED. RAMA'S ARMY REACHED LANKA. ON THE SEASHORE SURROUNDING THE CITY, THE ARMY SET UP CAMP.

SOME RAKSHASAS CAME TO RAMA'S CAMP DISGUISED AS MONKEYS.

HOW MANY MEN DO WE HAVE IN THE NORTH?

BUT VIBHEESHANA HAD SEEN THROUGH THEIR DISGUISE.

WHO IS LEADING THE SOUTH ATTACK?

HANU-MAN AND LAXMANA!

THESE ARE SPIES! SHALL WE KILL THEM?

NO, LET THEM GO. LET THEM TELL RAVANA WHAT HIS ENEMY IS LIKE!

PRINCE RAMA IS SO GENEROUS!

BEFORE THE BATTLE, RAVANA WENT TO A TOWER TO SURVEY THE ENEMY.

IN THE CENTRE THE CHARIOT BELONGS TO RAMA. INDRA GAVE IT TO HIM. TO HIS LEFT IS SUGREEVA!

HA! WE SHALL KILL THEM ALL!

THE BATTLE STARTED. THE MONKEYS ATTACKED WITH HUGE BOULDERS.

THE RAKSHASA GENERAL JAMBUMALI CAME TO FIGHT WITH HANUMAN. HANUMAN SMASHED HIS CHARIOT.

HANUMAN LIFTED RAMA AND LAXMANA TO HIS SHOULDERS. FROM THIS HIGH PERCH, THEIR ARROWS FOUND PERFECT MARKS.

DHUMRAKSHA CAME WITH A HUGE ARMY. HE WAS ONE OF RAVANA'S BEST GENERALS.

HANUMAN LIFTED HIM IN ONE HAND AND KILLED HIM.

NEXT TO COME WAS THE VICIOUS GIANT AKAMPANA. THE VANARAS RAN AWAY AT THE SIGHT OF HIM.

DON'T RUN AWAY! DON'T BE AFRAID!

HANUMAN UPROOTED A TREE AND KILLED AKAMPANA. HUNDREDS OF RAKSHASAS DIED CRUSHED BY THIS GIANT'S BODY.

WE MUST DESTROY THEM.

DO NOT WORRY, FATHER! I SHALL KILL THEM ALL! THEY CANNOT EVEN SEE ME.

AKAMPANA'S DEATH CAME AS A SHOCK TO RAVANA. MANY OF HIS GENERALS WERE DEAD. HIS GRIEF INCREASED HIS RAGE.

RAVANA'S SON INDRAJIT HAD RECEIVED A BOON FROM THE GODS. HE COULD FIGHT ANYONE WITHOUT BEING SEEN BY THE ENEMY.

LOOK! LAXMANA IS HIT BY AN ARROW!

WHEN THE BATTLE CEASED FOR THE DAY, (THEY NEVER FOUGHT AFTER SUNSET IN THOSE DAYS) ALL STOOD AROUND THE FALLEN LAXMANA, THEIR HEARTS HEAVY WITH GRIEF.

WHAT SHALL WE DO?

BRING THE PHYSICIAN.

HANUMAN RUSHED TO ANOTHER PART OF THE BATTLE FIELD WHERE HE FOUND SUSHENA.

WHERE ARE YOU TAKING ME?

YOU MUST CURE MY PRINCE!

I NEED SANJEEVANI PLANT TO CURE LAXMANA!

FAR AWAY ON THE GANDHAMADAN HILL STOOD THE SANJEEVANI TREE. ITS ROOT COULD BRING LAXMANA BACK TO LIFE. BRAVE HANUMAN STARTED ON ANOTHER LEAP.

HANUMAN COULD NOT LOCATE THE TREE FROM AMONGST HUNDRED OTHERS. BUT THERE WAS VERY LITTLE TIME.

WHICH IS THE SANJEEVANI TREE?

UNWILLING TO WASTE ANY MORE TIME, HANUMAN GREW IN SIZE AND LIFTED THE WHOLE MOUNTAIN IN HIS HANDS AND RETURNED TO LANKA.

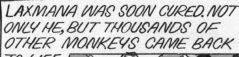
LAXMANA WAS SOON CURED. NOT ONLY HE, BUT THOUSANDS OF OTHER MONKEYS CAME BACK TO LIFE.

AS THE BATTLE STARTED AGAIN, RAVANA CAME OUT TO FIGHT IN HIS GOLDEN CHARIOT, HIS CROWN DAZZLING IN THE SUNLIGHT.

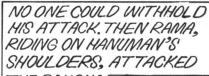
NO ONE COULD WITHHOLD HIS ATTACK. THEN RAMA, RIDING ON HANUMAN'S SHOULDERS, ATTACKED THE RAKSHA-SA KING.

RAMA'S ARROW CUT DOWN RAVANA'S CHARIOT. HE STOOD ON THE BATTLE GROUND, FACING DEATH.

YOU MAY GO NOW! I SHALL NOT KILL AN UNARMED ENEMY!

THE COUNCIL OF WAR IN RAVANA'S COURT.

WHO IS TO LEAD THE ARMY?

WAKE UP KU-MBHAKARNA!

KUMBHAKARNA USED TO SLEEP FOR SIX MONTHS AT A STRETCH.

PLEASE WAKE UP.

AT LAST, THE GIANT'S SLEEP WAS BROKEN.

WHAT IS THE MATTER?

YOU MUST GO TO BATTLE.

LIKE A TYPHOON, KUMBHAKARNA CAME TO THE BATTLE. THOUSANDS PERISHED UNDER HIS FEET.

RAMA'S ARROWS CUT HIS HEAD OFF.

RAVANA HAS NOBODY ELSE TO FIGHT FOR HIM.

INDRAJIT HAS GONE TO OFFER A SACRIFICE.

IF INDRAJIT COULD COMPLETE HIS SACRIFICIAL PRAYER, HE WOULD BECOME INVINCIBLE. BUT HIS PRAYER WAS NOT COMPLETED.

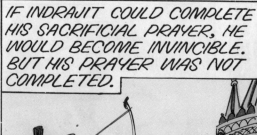

WHEN THE NEWS OF INDRAJIT'S DEATH REACHED RAVANA—

I AM ALL ALONE NOW! BUT I'M STILL THE MIGHTIEST.

IT WAS TIME FOR THE LAST BATTLE. RAVANA CAME TO THE GATES OF LANKA. OUTSIDE, THE VANARA ARMY WAITED.

RAVANA RODE ON HIS CHARIOT, LIKE LIGHTNING, TEARING THROUGH THE RANKS OF THE VANARA ARMY.

RAVANA WAS A GREAT WARRIOR. THE BATTLE THAT RAGED WAS FIERCE.

AT LAST RAVANA CAME FACE TO FACE WITH RAMA. RAMA PICKED UP HIS BOW FOR THE LAST ARROW OF THIS GREAT BATTLE.

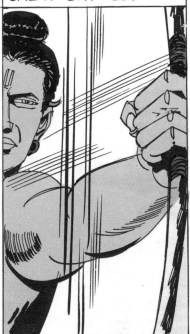

THE EVIL ENEMY HAD BEEN DESTROYED. VIRTUE HAD WON OVER GREED AND LUST.

THE KING HAD DIED. THE CITY OF LANKA WAS DARK AND MOURNFUL.

VIBHEESHANA WAS CROWNED THE KING OF LANKA.

SOON THE TRIUMPHAL MARCH BEGAN, OVER THE OCEAN, THE WAY THEY HAD COME.

COME MY BELOVED! YOU CAME IN THIS FLYING CHARIOT IN DISGRACE! YOU SHALL RETURN IN HONOUR!

AT LAST IT WAS TIME FOR RAMA'S RETURN TO AYODHYA. HANUMAN WENT AHEAD WITH THE NEWS.

I BRING HAPPY TIDINGS! FOURTEEN YEARS OF EXILE ARE OVER. THE MASTER IS COMING HOME.

THE WHOLE CITY ASSEMBLED TO WELCOME THE RETURNING PRINCES. THERE WAS JOY ALL AROUND.

LONG LIVE KING RAMA!

LONG LIVE PRINCE LAXMANA!

LONG LIVE QUEEN SITA!

The Sons of
Rama

AMAR CHITRA KATHA

Illustrated Classics From India

The Sons of Rama

Sage Valmiki first set down the story of Rama and Sita in his epic poem, Ramayana.

Rama was the eldest son of Dasharatha, the king of Ayodhya, who had three wives – Kausalya, Kaikeyi and Sumitra. Rama was the son of Kausalya, Bharata of Kaikeyi and Lazmana and Shatrughna of Sumitra. The four princes grew up to be brave and valiant. Rama won the hand of Sita, the daughter of King Janaka. Dasharatha wanted to crown Rama as the king but Kaikeyi objected. Using boons granted to her by Dasharatha earlier, she had Rama banished to the forest. Sita and Laxmana decided to follow Rama. While in the forest, a Rakshasi, Shoorpanakha, accosted Laxmana but had her nose cut off by him. In revenge, her brother Ravana, king of Lanka, carried Sita away. Rama and Laxmana set out to look for her and with the help of an army of monkeys, they defeated Ravana.

When they returned to Ayodhya after fourteen years in exile, Rama banished Sita on the suspicions of his subjects. She found refuge in the ashrama of sage Valmiki where she gave birth to twin sons, Luv and Kush.

This Amar Chitra Katha title is based on Uttara-Ramacharita of Bhavabhuti.

Illustrations: Pratap Mulick   Cover: Pratap Mulick

THE SONS OF RAMA

RAMA WAS THE KING OF AYODHYA. PEOPLE WERE HAPPY AND PROSPEROUS UNDER HIS RULE.

WITH HIS BROTHERS, LAXMANA, BHARATA AND SHATRUGHNA, RAMA USED TO VISIT HIS PEOPLE AND LISTEN TO THEIR PROBLEMS...

... AND EVERY EVENING WITH HIS QUEEN SITA, HE RECEIVED HIS MEN. ONE EVENING —

SPEAK UP; YOU HAVE NOTHING TO FEAR!

SIRE, I CANNOT! NOT IN THE PRESENCE OF THE QUEEN!

MAHARAJ, TODAY A LAUNDERER WAS BEATING HIS WIFE, AND HE SAID...

GET OUT OF MY HOUSE! I'M NOT LIKE RAMA WHO ACCEPTS A WIFE AFTER SHE HAS LIVED IN ANOTHER'S HOUSE!

SHOULD I TURN MY WIFE OUT BECAUSE OF WHAT THE LAUNDERER SAID? NO... NO... AND SHE IS SOON TO BECOME A MOTHER!

BUT MY FIRST DUTY IS TOWARDS MY PEOPLE... I HAVE TO SEND HER AWAY...

THE FOLLOWING DAY HE SENT FOR LAXMANA.

YOU WILL TAKE SITA INTO THE JUNGLES AND LEAVE HER THERE.

BUT...

NO BUTS, THIS IS MY DECISION!

LAXMANA GOT HIS CHARIOT READY...

...AND LEFT AYODHYA FOR THE FOREST.

LAXMANA, THIS JUNGLE IS SO FRIGHTENING. I'M SCARED!

HOW CAN I LEAVE HER IN THIS WILD JUNGLE? BUT I MUST OBEY RAMA'S COMMAND!

AFTER LAXMANA LEFT FOR AYODHYA, SITA WAS ALONE IN THE JUNGLE.

WHERE SHALL I GO?

JUST THEN A SERPENT APPEARED.

HELP! HELP!

DON'T WORRY MY CHILD— THESE ANIMALS ARE FROM MY HERMITAGE.

MAHARSHI VALMIKI! IT'S YOU!

VALMIKI TOOK SITA TO HIS HERMITAGE.

YOU WILL LIVE HERE. NOTHING WILL BOTHER YOU!

VALMIKI'S HERMITAGE BECAME SITA'S HAVEN— SHE WAS BLESSED WITH TWIN SONS.

LUV DEAR, WHERE IS KUSH?

HERE I AM, MOTHER, BOXING THIS DEER'S EARS!

BUT THE MAHARSHI TAUGHT YOU NOT TO BE CRUEL TO ANIMALS!

IT WAS THE DEER WHO WAS BEING CRUEL TO ME!

MAHARSHI VALMIKI PERSONALLY ATTENDED TO THEIR EDUCATION.

HE TAUGHT THEM THE USE OF ARMS AS WELL.

PULL WITH ALL YOUR MIGHT, THEN LET THE ARROW GO.

LUV AND KUSH PRACTISED WHAT THEY WERE TAUGHT EVERY DAY.

WHAT'S THIS? ARE YOU TWO TRYING TO KILL EACH OTHER?

NOT AT ALL, MOTHER! WE ARE PRACTISING HOW TO STAY EACH OTHER'S ARROWS.

LET'S GO. IT'S TIME FOR DINNER!

VALMIKI TOLD THEM THE STORY OF THE RAMAYANA, OF HOW RAMA BROKE THE BOW OF LORD SHIVA AND MARRIED VAIDEHI.

THAT IS NOTHING. I CAN ALSO BREAK A BOW.

"KAIKEYI BANISHED RAMA INTO THE JUNGLES FOR FOURTEEN YEARS."

I'M GOING INTO THE JUNGLES TO KEEP MY FATHER'S PROMISE!

I WANT TO GO WITH YOU!

"ONE DAY AS RAMA WENT AFTER A DEER, RAVANA KIDNAPPED VAIDEHI.

"IN THE BATTLE THAT FOLLOWED, RAVANA WAS KILLED BY RAMA."

VICTORY TO RAMA!

"AFTER SPENDING FOURTEEN YEARS IN EXILE, RAMA RETURNED TO AYODHYA AND WAS CROWNED KING."

ONE DAY, BECAUSE OF WHAT A LAUNDERER SAID, RAMA BANISHED VAIDEHI!

POOR VAIDEHI! RAMA WAS CRUEL, INDEED!

VALMIKI TAUGHT THEM OF "YAJNA" AND SUCH OTHER MATTERS TOO.

"SWAHA"

"SWAHA"

"SWAHA"

EVERY DAY THEY PRACTISED THE ARTS OF WAR. THEY ALSO TALKED ABOUT VAIDEHI.

I WONDER WHAT HAPPENED TO VAIDEHI?

IF EVER WE MEET HER, WE'LL BRING HER TO THE HERMITAGE.

THEY DID NOT REALISE THAT VAIDEHI WAS NONE OTHER THAN SITA, THEIR MOTHER.

MEANWHILE, IN AYODHYA RAMA PREPARED TO PERFORM THE ASHWAMEDHA YAJNA.

AS PEOPLE PASSED BY HIS ROYAL PALACE—

KING RAMA WILL NOW BECOME A WORLD CONQUEROR.

ALL WERE INVITED TO THE YAJNA.

THE GREAT SAGES, VISHWA-MITRA AND NARADA ARE HERE TOO.

THEY ARE STAYING WITH THE SAGE VASHISHTHA.

RULERS FROM ALL AROUND CAME WITH THEIR ARMIES.

WHAT HAVE THESE ARMIES TO DO WITH A YAJNA?

THEY HAVE COME JUST TO WITNESS IT AND, IF NEED BE, TO FIGHT ON THE SIDE OF RAMA.

THE YAJNASHALA WAS DECORATED; PREPARATIONS WERE NOW COMPLETE.

BUT NARADA HAD SOMETHING TO SAY TO VISHWAMITRA.

HOW CAN RAMA PERFORM THE YAJNA WITHOUT HIS WIFE SITA?

HE WILL HAVE TO USE A GOLDEN STATUE OF HER!

A WHITE HORSE WITH BLACK EARS WAS GOT READY FOR THE YAJNA.

THE HORSE IS MAGNIFICENT!

EXCELLENT ARRANGEMENTS. EXCEPT FOR SITA'S ABSENCE.

THE MENTION OF SITA SET RAMA THINKING.

I SHOULD SEND LAXMANA TO LOOK FOR SITA.

NO, MY PEOPLE MAY NOT LIKE IT. A GOLDEN STATUE WILL HAVE TO DO!

VISHWAMITRA TIED THE CEREMONIAL GOLD LEAF ON THE HORSE'S FOREHEAD.

THE HORSE WAS THEN LET LOOSE AND THE ARMY FOLLOWED IT.

AS THE HORSE ENTERED A RULER'S DOMAIN—

WHAT SHALL WE DO, MY MINISTER?

WE CAN'T DO ANYTHING. WE ARE TOO WEAK. EVEN RAVANA WAS NO MATCH FOR RAMA.

MANY A RULER ACCEPTED RAMA'S SUPREMACY WITHOUT A FIGHT.

NOBODY CHECKS THE HORSE.

WHO DARES FIGHT THIS ARMY?

LUV AND KUSH SAW THE HORSE FROM AFAR.

KUSH, LET'S CATCH THAT HORSE!

LOOK AT THIS, LUV. ANYONE WHO HOLDS THIS HORSE WILL HAVE TO FIGHT!

THEN WE WILL FIGHT!

LUV AND KUSH TIED THE HORSE TO A TREE.

ONE OF RAMA'S SOLDIERS CAME UP TO THEM.

CHILDREN! GIVE THAT HORSE BACK TO ME!

SHAME ON YOU FOR BEGGING.

AND A TERRIBLE BATTLE FOLLOWED.

ONE OF THE SOLDIERS HASTENED BACK TO SHATRUGHNA.

SIRE! THOSE TWO CHILDREN ARE IMPOSSIBLE! THEY HAVE MADE FOOLS OF US!

I'LL TEACH THEM HOW TO BEHAVE!

HE'S VERY PROUD OF HIS CHARIOT!

WE'LL SHOW HIM!

LUV, SHOOT AT THE WHEEL!

H-E-R-E GOES!

JUST ONE SHOT TOOK CARE OF HIM!

AS SHATRUGHNA FELL, RAMA'S ARMY FLED IN DISARRAY.

I'VE LOST A SHOE!

I HAVE LOST MY SWORD!

SOME OF THE SOLDIERS WENT UP TO RAMA.

VICTORY TO RAMA. TWO YOUNG BOYS... JUST TWO OF THEM...

YES SIRE, THEY MADE HIM FALL FROM HIS CHARIOT!

SHATRUGHNA FALLEN!!

RAMA WAS DISTURBED.

TWO CHILDREN, AND SO BRAVE! WHO COULD THEY BE? YOU TAKE OVER, LAXMANA. GO AND CAPTURE THOSE BOYS.

I WILL GO AT ONCE!

LUV YOU STAY WITH THE HORSE; I'LL DEAL WITH HIM!

DON'T YOU WANT TO LIVE, LAD?

YOU BETTER PRAY FOR YOUR OWN LIFE!

AND KUSH SHOT AN ARROW...

...WHICH TOOK OFF WITH LAXMANA'S HELMET.

...THE SOLDIERS WHISPERED AMONGST THEMSELVES.

THEIR ARROWS SEEM TO FLY BY MAGIC!

WE SHOULD MAKE FRIENDS WITH THEM.

KUSH AND LAXMANA ENGAGED IN A FURIOUS BATTLE.

KUSH WAS WOUNDED IN THE FIGHT.

ENRAGED, LUV CHALLENGED LAXMANA TO A DUEL.

I WON'T LET YOU LIVE AFTER WHAT YOU HAVE DONE TO KUSH!

LUV HAD HIS REVENGE. LAXMANA FELL UNCONSCIOUS.

RUN FOR YOUR LIVES!

LAXMANA HAS FALLEN!

RAMA WAS VERY UPSET WHEN HE HEARD THE NEWS.

NOW BHARATA, YOU MUST GO WITH THE MONKEY FORCES.

AND THE MONKEYS PREPARED FOR BATTLE.

HANUMAN ALSO ACCOMPANIED BHARATA.

LUV AND KUSH EXCHANGED MEANINGFUL LOOKS.

SAY, LET'S MAKE MONKEYS OUT OF THESE MONKEYS!

THE SOONER THE BETTER!

INSTANTLY AN ARROW STRUCK HANUMAN'S MACE.

THESE BRATS DESERVE TO BE KILLED!

THE MONKEY FORCES WENT INTO ACTION AGAINST LUV AND KUSH...

...BUT PROVED UNEQUAL TO THE TASK.

BHARATA ALSO FELL AND HANUMAN HURRIED BACK TO RAMA.

A THOUSAND PARDONS, O RAMA!

DON'T LOSE HEART, HANUMAN. I WILL COME MYSELF.

RAMA LED HIS HUGE FORCES.

RAMA DECIDED TO FIND OUT ABOUT THE CHILDREN.

WHO ARE YOUR FATHER AND MOTHER?

WE DO NOT KNOW ABOUT OUR FATHER. BUT SITA IS OUR MOTHER. BUT WHY ARE YOU SO INTERESTED ANYWAY?

THOUGH THE BOYS DID NOT KNOW THIER FATHER, RAMA RECOGNISED THEM. HIS BOW DROPPED FROM HIS HANDS.

YOU ARE SITA'S...

LOOK, HE IS FAINTING! AND JUST BECAUSE OF WHAT WE SAID. LET'S GO AND TAKE CARE OF HIS ARMY.

SOON LUV AND KUSH HAD THE MONKEYS AT THEIR MERCY.

THEY TIED HANUMAN NEAR THE HORSE.

MOTHER WILL BE PLEASED TO SEE OUR CAPTIVE MONKEY!

THE MONKEYS DEALT WITH, LUV AND KUSH RETURNED TO RAMA.

GOODNESS! HE IS STILL UN- CONSCIOUS!

LET'S TAKE AWAY HIS CROWN.

HANUMAN WAS STILL TIED UP.

WON'T YOU EVER UNTIE ME, BOYS?

SAY WITH ME, GLORY BE TO RAMA!

VALMIKI BROUGHT SITA FORWARD.

YOU MUST TAKE SITA BACK WITH YOU.

MAHARSHI, HAVING ONCE SENT HER AWAY, HOW CAN I...

SITA COULD NOT BEAR THE HUMILIATION ANY MORE.

MOTHER EARTH, IF I AM PURE, GATHER ME TO YOUR LAP!

...AND THE EARTH PARTED UNDER HER FEET...

MOVE AWAY, MOTHER! THE EARTH IS FALLING APART!

YOU HAVE GRANTED MY WISH, O MOTHER.

...AND SITA BEGAN TO SINK IN.

MOTHER! MOTHER!

RAMA EMBRACED HIS ANGUISHED SONS.

DO NOT GRIEVE MY SONS. YOUR MOTHER HAS GONE BACK TO HER MOTHER.

IT WAS SAID, SITA WAS BORN OF THE EARTH. THIS PROBABLY WAS TRUE.